THE ART OF LIVING
BETWEEN HELL
AND BREAKFAST

DILLON GARRISON

A Morningside Publishing Book
Payson, Arizona

The Art of Living Between Hell and Breakfast is a work of fiction. Names, characters, places, brands, media, and incidents are either the product of the author's imagination or are used fictitiously. Any resemblance to actual persons living or dead, events, or locales is entirely coincidental. The author acknowledges the trademarked status and trademark owners of various products referenced in this work of fiction, which have been used without permission. The publication/use of these trademarks is not authorized, associated with, or sponsored by the trademark owners.

The Art of Living Between Hell and Breakfast

A Morningside Publishing Book

Text Copyright © 2016 by Val Edward Simone
All Rights Reserved.

Printed in the United States of America

Library of Congress Control Number: 2016916737

Printed Version
ISBN 978-1-936210-62-6

Cover Design: Val Edward Simone

For more books please visit:
www.morningsidepublishing.com
www.ekidslandpublishing.com

MORNINGSIDE
PUBLISHING, LLC
PAYSON, ARIZONA

Dedication:
To the artists

With Special Thanks To:
Editor
Rita Samols

Musical Inspiration
Ernesto Cortazar II
Kevin Kern
Secret Garden
R. Carlos Nakai

CHAPTER 1

Fort Sill, Oklahoma
November 1908

"There is an art to living between Hell and breakfast, and we are the artists. We create the artwork on the canvas that is our life."

"How about dyin', Geronimo? Is there an art to that as well?" asked Kansas City reporter Gerald C. Thompson.

Geronimo did not answer the question immediately. Instead, he gazed skyward and studied the thickening gray clouds massing above them. It was going to snow soon. It was a very chilly day, and the storm threatened to be a big one.

The other natives sat quietly in front of their fires, with nothing to do except prepare to sit out the coming storm as best they could.

The Army gave them rations, but they were meager and never enough. There was nothing the proud people could do to aid in their own survival but to sit and pray, and wish that they were free.

Geronimo sat on the ground in front of his own fire, wrapped in a blanket not woven by the women of his tribe and decorated with colorful Apache artwork. His blanket had been made in a mill somewhere back east and had the words U.S. ARMY stenciled in white across it.

Gerald Thompson studied the blanket. The stencil was printed on both sides in the center of all four edges, so no matter which way it was wrapped around the wearer, the words were visible across the back and neck.

Thompson wondered if the name of the blanket's owner was printed that way as a reminder of whose will it was that pressed heavily upon the necks of the conquered — a reminder of who was now master.

Geronimo seemed oblivious to the type of blanket it was or the placement of the printing and the message it revealed to an observer like a scab-picking reporter seeking a sensational article to send back to his anxious publisher. Or perhaps it was simply fatalistic acquiescence that kept such thoughts away.

But it seemed to keep him warm, and he appeared content with that small favor.

His old, tired eyes dropped down from the sky to the fire, where he seemed to study the flames. But he soon lifted his worn-out but still clear eyes and smiled graciously at the foolish man who sat beside him, eagerly awaiting his response, pencil in hand hovering anxiously over his notepad.

"There *is* an art to how we die. We create *that* artwork on the canvas that is our spirit before we cross over to the other world. It is our task during our walk through life to become true artists, so that we can create the good art of dying — sometime, we hope, after breakfast."

"How about you, then, sir? Are you a good artist?"

"It is not for us to judge our work as artists, Mister Thompson. That judgment is for the artists who follow after we are gone.

"During my walk through this life I have learned many ways to create the art of living. I have also learned many ways to create the art of dying. I am not sure which of my art will be the best when my walk is ended."

Geronimo lifted his eyes skyward again and stared silently, as if searching for a secret wisdom hidden up in the firmament somewhere above the gathering clouds. Then he turned his eyes once more toward the reporter.

"When I was younger, I met a White-Eye whose heart was on fire with a great hate. The flames consumed him very much. I think even his spirit burned.

"I spent as much time as I could with him and I tried to show him how to live peacefully with the hate. It was not easy to do. The flames were very hot.

"I understood the heat of his hate, for I have felt that same fire burning in me. And those who have walked through the fire rarely speak kindly of the flames."

"No, sir, Geronimo. I don't imagine they would, bein' hot like that and all."

Geronimo answered graciously, ignoring the reporter's ineptness. "You do not understand my words, Mister Thompson."

"No, I don't suppose I do. I can't say that I'm all that familiar with that sort of burning, Geronimo. But tell me this. It's been many years since you've been on the warpath against the army and all. Do you still harbor a great hate for the army?"

"I am too old now to carry hate in my heart. Hate is very heavy for an old man."

"How about rage? Do you still feel a fiery rage for the wrongs done to you?"

"I do not feel rage anymore. That burden is too great also. But you wish me to feel rage, do you not? You would sell more newspapers if you could write that I am still the angry, savage Indian your readers want me to be. Is this not true?"

"Well, I won't lie to ya, sir. I'd sell more papers with you sayin' that, rather than you tellin' me that you're now tamed of spirit and mind. But you ain't, though, are ya? Tamed, I mean. They ain't kilt off the last of that feisty Injun spirit, have they?"

"I hold no more spirit for war and anger, for hate and rage," said Geronimo. "I sent those spirits away a very long time ago. I cannot say it was easy for me to lose the hate or to quiet the rage for what I have suffered at the hands of the Mexicans and the Blue-Coats, but as I said, I am old now. I need more sleep than I used to. The raging spirits that once danced in my head at night, keeping me angry and restless, I had to send them back into the dark place from where they came. I think, in the end, even they had grown tired of their weight."

"You speak English very well, Geronimo."

"It is important to speak the language of those who hold you prisoner."

"Why?"

"So you know when they lie to you."

"Do they lie to you?"

"The Blue-Coats have always lied to my people."

"How do you feel about that?"

"I am a prisoner, Mister Thompson. It does not matter how I feel about it anymore."

"So, you're tellin' me that you're beat? The army has done beat all the fight outa ya? Is that what you're tellin' me?"

"When a man is young, as I was long ago, the evil ones battle for the prize of his fresh spirit."

"The evil ones?"

"The dark spirits who live in the shadowlands."

"Ah, I see. Okay."

"For a while they are strong, and they make the young man's heart yearn for the thrill and glory of the fight. His eyes see only a fine and noble struggle before them — a prize to be won, a foe to be conquered, a great endeavor to be accomplished.

"I like that word, *endeavor*. The President said it to me once. He said, 'I hope that you shall endeavor to become great.' I liked what he said. But I said to him, 'I am already great, but I shall endeavor to become greater.' He laughed. We both laughed. It was good to laugh. I like him."

"Geronimo, excuse me, but you were talkin' about bein' young and the glory of a fight," the pushy reporter prodded. "Could you say more about that?"

Geronimo looked into the reporter's eyes for a moment and then smiled.

"For a woman's spirit or for a noble cause, there is no difference to a young man's heart which seeks to conquer. To that heart, all battles are the same. And the promise of more glorious battles to come keeps his heart full of fire.

"But when a man becomes old, as I am now, he looks upon the battles differently. He measures more the loss against victory. His heart understands that losing a fight is not admitting defeat, but losing the lives of his people for no good cause is a battle bitterly lost — a defeat too bitter to bear. He comes to understand that sometimes a great victory can be won by not fighting at all. And he learns that a greater glory can be achieved in seeing the smile of a child who no longer lives in fear."

"So you see your surrender as a victory, then?"

"I did not surrender, Mister Thompson. I chose the lives of my people over my selfish desire to do battle with the Blue-Coats. My heart learned the difference between sweetness and bitterness. It chose the sweetness of life over the bitterness of death."

Geronimo opened his mouth and stuck out his tongue to catch a floating snowflake.

"My tongue is the same as my heart. It, too, knows sweetness and bitterness. I think it prefers the sweetness of a snowflake to the bitterness of the dirt of the grave."

Geronimo pulled the army-issued gray wool blanket tighter around his shoulders and looked skyward again.

"I have seen nearly eighty winters, Mister Thompson. Each winter seems colder than the last. Maybe they are, or maybe I am just thinner and older and cannot take the cold as I did when I was younger. Anyway, they feel colder. I do not think I will see many more winters. I am hearing the call of the next life. The call is becoming louder with each passing day. Soon, I think, it will be too loud for me to ignore."

"Geronimo, please forgive me, but I've come a long way to interview you. You just gotta know my publisher is after a stirrin' story, sir."

"My story is now only one of great sadness. Would you like to hear of the sadness that lives in my heart? There is also a terrible regret. Would your readers like to hear of my great regret?"

"To be honest, my publisher wants to know about the great hate and rage, but he did ask me to inquire of you how you're adaptin' to life here after so many years in Florida. Could you talk some about that, please?"

"When I was in Florida, I looked up to the sky. I saw that it was the same sky there as it is here, except that in Florida it does not snow. I saw no change in the seasons. I could not tell a summer moon from a winter moon in the night sky. But I tell you this. Now that I am back here, very near to the land of my ancestors, the moon remains the same to me.

"The great fellow up there stares down at me still and laughs. He continues to mock me for choosing a disgraceful life over an honorable death — for allowing myself to stop walking and be captured by the Blue-Coats, for allowing them to take away our way of life. He calls me fool. But I do not like his words. I shout back at him and tell him so, but his face does not change and his voice still calls me a fool. And perhaps that should become my fate. Perhaps I should be remembered as a fool who walked in the darkness of his bad choices. I am not free, for I did not shout loud enough, I did not fight hard enough, I did not believe strong enough in the honor of the old ways to remain free.

"I chose life for my people, but I know now that I have failed them all, because life without freedom is as a bad death – dark, empty, and full of regret. And in the darkness created by poor choices is where fools gather and wait for death to come to them. But even as a fool living in the midst of such darkness, I shall never surrender the light that shines within."

"But what if you could? You know, fight like the dickens again?" the reporter asked. "What then? What do ya think?"

"At my age, I do not think like a young man. If I could become young again, I would do what I did before — fight and kill and shout in a loud voice my great rage against both the Mexicans and the Blue-Coats. But then I ask myself if, after I grew old once more, would I allow myself to be captured again as I did? This is a question that I have been seeking to answer lately, but I cannot find the answer in my heart, in my mind, or in my spirit. I ask Usen, our Apache god, for an answer with a loud voice. But Usen does not answer me. Maybe I shall never receive the answer I seek. Maybe there will be no more answers for me on this walk. Maybe the answer is that I should stop asking my silly questions and die quietly in the shame that was my capture."

Thompson wrote down every word Geronimo spoke, with the express hope of later turning them around and making them more frightful for his readers. Turn them around he would have to do, because he did not see any frightening words on his notepad.

Finally, he looked at Geronimo through desperate eyes. "Isn't there *anything* you can tell me, Geronimo, that would make an excitin' story for my readers?"

Geronimo looked skyward once again, and once more caught a falling snowflake on his tongue.

He closed his steely, piercing eyes and sat silently and still for several long moments.

Thompson studied the old man as he sat with his eyes closed, and he could detect no fierceness in the calm face of the Apache chief. He did not see the hideous glare that had once caused women to shriek with unrelenting terror. He did not see the awful scowl that had once brought brave men to their knees in dreadful fright. He saw before him only a troubled old Indian — a man of captured countenance, seized spirit, and wretched resignation, stained with a hint of remembered hope. A man living with a great sorrow in his soul. A man who, although defeated by the U.S. Army, had conquered his own demons long before allowing himself to be captured. A man who, sitting amongst the falling snowflakes, had successfully subjugated his warring nature and was now carefully measuring the results of all his follies against the gloomy peace pressing mercilessly against his wounded heart. A man hiding all the haunting discomforts of indignation he had ever suffered behind that warm, crooked, friendly smile.

The old man was different from anyone he had ever interviewed before, choosing to sit out under the falling snow on a blanket by a fire instead of inside his government-provided home of mud-brick and wood — choosing to sit as he had when he was once, long ago now, a free man.

In that small, seemingly insignificant choice, Gerald Thompson recognized the spark of rebellion still smoldering within the proud Apache chief.

Geronimo finally opened his eyes and stared at Thompson. "You want a story about rage?"

"I do, sir. Yes, very much. Something really excitin'."

"I told you about the White-Eye I knew long ago who was on fire with a great hate. Do you remember those words?"

"Yes, I believe I do," replied Thompson as he thumbed through his notes. "Yes. Here it is. He's the one you tried to help. Is that the man?"

"Yes. Would you like to read the story about him?"

"At this point, sir, I'll take any excitin' story you wish to tell me."

"I will not *tell* you the story. It is not my story to tell. But I have the story in a book. He visited me six months ago and gave it to me."

Geronimo arose gingerly from his blanket and ambled into his home, struggling against the pain in his knees and hips — pain born in the many hard years on the prairie hiding and running from the U.S. Army. That kind of life, lived under those arduous conditions, would bring any man to pain-filled days later in life, if he was lucky enough to live that long.

Geronimo returned with a leather-bound, handwritten journal. He handed it to the reporter and agonizingly sat down again on his blanket by the fire.

"This is the story of the man. He wrote it down. He read it to me. See here, on this page," said Geronimo proudly, opening the journal to the first page. "He made his mark here. It was a gift to me."

Thompson took the journal from Geronimo's hands and looked at the opened page. It read, *One Man's Journey Toward Understanding the Art of Living Between Hell and Breakfast.*

Under the title was the handwritten inscription: *To my friend, Goyahkla. The stiller of my raging soul. Connor Beckett.*

"Connor Beckett?" said Thompson. "I've heard the name. Is he by chance related to the famous John Kendall Beckett, the former Texas Ranger?"

Geronimo nodded. "His son."

"Yeah. I believe John Beckett now owns a sizeable ranch down there in Texas along the Brazos. I didn't know he had a son who was an author. And this looks to be an original handwritten copy."

"It is the story you asked for," said Geronimo. "It is a very exciting story, about murder, rage, betrayal, revenge, and redemption. All the things your readers in Kansas City will want to read about, I think."

The old Indian stared out into space once more and fell quiet.

After a time, Thompson leaned in toward Geronimo. "Is there something else, Geronimo?"

The old man blinked his eyes.

"*Redemption.* I like that word very much. Connor Beckett said it was a good word to know. He said redemption is like paying a debt. Once you have paid what you owe, you will be free again. I wonder if I can pay what I owe to my people and be free again. Do you think I can pay my debt of betrayal?"

"I don't know anything about that, Geronimo."

"If I pay that, will I be able to return to the land of my ancestors — to walk through the grass as I once did in my younger years — to speak to the old fellow in the moon again as a man and not as a fool — to feel my spirit fly again?"

"I'm afraid I can't answer those questions, Geronimo."

"I do not seek answers from you, Mister Thompson. No one can answer my questions. They are for me to ask and for me to answer."

"But this journal is wonderful," stated the reporter, skimming through it. "May I take it with me, to read back at the hotel? I'll give it back to you before I leave."

"You may not take it with you. You may read it there," replied Geronimo, pointing to a chair under the dilapidated roof of the ramada.

"Fine, sir. Just as you say."

Geronimo nodded knowingly. He knew well it would keep the pesky reporter occupied for a good long while. "It is a great story about a great man," he said. "It is about my friend and *his* battle with the dark spirits who wanted to destroy him — to destroy everything he was, to keep him crazy. It is a fine story of how he discovered the path to *his* redemption, *his* freedom."

Geronimo looked up into the sky again, as if searching for a sweet memory stored somewhere among the stars. He found it and retrieved it, yet he remained quiet and still for several more minutes as he gathered other faraway reclaimed treasures.

Thompson cleared his throat to regain Geronimo's attention.

Geronimo glanced at Thompson and smiled the crooked smile that was his trademark. His eyes sparkled with the recaptured memories.

Thompson returned his look. "Is there something more? Do you have other thoughts?"

"I have many thoughts, Mister Thompson, but these thoughts are only for me."

"As you wish, of course. May I? Read the journal, I mean? May I begin now?"

Geronimo nodded.

"Thank you." Thompson stood up and walked toward the house.

Under the cover of the ramada, protected now from the falling snow, he seated himself in the chair and glanced once more at Geronimo, seated on his blanket next to the fire, smiling mysteriously at an invisible vision before him.

Then he opened the journal and began to read.

CHAPTER 2

Tombstone, Arizona
1885

Connor Beckett's massive six-foot-four-inch frame had sat squashed into the barroom chair for more than two hours. It was a chair designed for much smaller men, a size more normal for men of that time.

Some found his size intimidating, stirring unwanted challenges, but his friendly smile and easy manner usually neutralized any disagreement or challenge quickly. In fact, most of the near brawls ended peaceably, with a friendly handshake and a broad smile on both faces.

That day, thankfully, had seen no challenges; indeed, it had been a restful, revitalizing day. He was relaxing and reading several back issues of the *Record-Epitaph*, one of Tombstone's two daily newspapers, until it was time to head home.

A feeling of urgency abruptly swept over him. It was like a dousing of ice water. He shivered. And all of a sudden, he became very anxious to get back home to his family. He couldn't understand why, but the pull to rush home was overwhelming.

Something was wrong, but he could not figure out what it was that had him so alarmed. Nausea churned his gut. He felt bile rising in his throat, but he held it back.

He rushed out of the saloon and stuffed the partially read newspaper into a saddlebag. He leapt up onto his palomino mare, Tilly, and reined her hard in the direction of his ranch, heeling her firmly as an urging to get going quickly.

Now, with the town of Tombstone disappearing behind him, Connor Beckett sat nervously in the saddle of his gallant, strong horse riding back to his ranch, the Double T Bar.

It was much too far and hot to gallop home; he'd kill Tilly with the effort. So he urged her to trot, knowing that she could not keep up the pace for very long in the midst of the sweltering afternoon heat, but also knowing that if he could keep on stride, he'd be within easy eyesight of his ranch well before his normal arrival time and sitting at the supper table surrounded by his loving family soon after that.

Twenty minutes later, the sense of rush and consternation subsided abruptly and soon thereafter disappeared altogether. He was suddenly relaxed, not understanding why such a feeling of urgency had overwhelmed him before. He thought it strange, but soon even that thought was gone.

He then felt excitement.

Tucked away in his saddlebags, along with the gifts for his family, were nineteen other back issues of the August 1885 *Record-Epitaph* for devouring later. Connor Beckett was an avid reader, with an inordinate predilection for all things of a scribal nature.

Getting into town once a month was like a child entering the finest candy store. As soon as his boots hit the dirt street, they were aimed in the direction of his favorite general store, specifically the section where Mr. Bernard, the store's proprietor, stacked the latest-to-arrive novels from New York and back issues of the newspaper.

Connor grabbed the novels, as many as he could afford, and savored the moment when, after a hard day's work on the ranch and after dinner, he could sit on the ramada next to the lantern and delve into worlds he could only ever know through those printed words, as well as catch up on the news of the area through those back editions of the newspaper.

Transveyance was the word Connor had coined to describe what he experienced when he read the novels. That is what words were to him — a miracle of transveyance. They were more than a conveyance, something merely transmitted. Transveyance was something more intimate. It was an *intimate conveyance* of wondrous images — something special, shared between them, the words and he, but without the need for the words themselves. It was more like a sharing between soul mates. As transveyors of intimate knowledge, filled with sacred words to be adored — a soul mate to his writist's enamored spirit, that's what books had become to him.

He read every day. He wrote stories on some occasions. And all the reading material that he had amassed on that particular trip to town would be scrupulously consumed by the time he made his next monthly sojourn back into town.

Under normal conditions, saddle time between town and his ranch gave him added opportunity to read. Along the way, he devoured every word of the *Record-Epitaph*'s earliest unread edition. And despite the content, the same mindless sensational exposition of otherwise normal events, he enjoyed knowing of current events that might affect him. His keen mind could quickly differentiate *sensational* drivel from *informational* significance.

Although each edition was expected to be different, he was never surprised to see basically the same information day after day. After all was said and done, the news was much the same each day anyway. These days, life in and around Tombstone was rarely surprising and different.

These days were calm when compared to the wild days of the past few years — the hectic days of the rich silver strikes that had brought Tombstone into existence. The savage times when the Earp brothers were at war with the cowboys, and the confusing days surrounding the bloody conclusion to their battles back in 1881, the *Gunfight on Fremont Street*, as the Tombstone Epitaph, the predecessor to the Record-Epitaph, had labeled it, or the devastating fires that destroyed almost every building and nearly killed off the town back in 1882.

Of late, however, the town seemed to have finally settled into the mundane, the usual — an uninspired, almost boring existence.

In the latest edition of the *Record-Epitaph*, the one he had just read, an article reported that Geronimo had once again made a daring breakout from the San Carlos Reservation with three other chiefs and 134 other Apaches: 42 braves and the rest women, children, and the elderly. But they had broken up into smaller bands and were skillfully avoiding any contact with the army.

Connor chuckled, for this was beginning to become another *normal* event for the surrounding area. The old, worn-out Indian just wouldn't stay put. His constant breakouts had been a running joke throughout the area for the longest time, but no one was laughing about it anymore because the article went on to report that Geronimo's band had killed a family near Silver City, New Mexico. They were now believed to be coming back through the Tombstone area in a daring dash southward toward Mexico.

In another article, the Thaddaeus "Cutter" Brown Gang had pulled off a stunning bank robbery in Tucson a few days before. The alert had spread far and wide quickly, requesting everyone to be on the lookout for the gang, now believed to also be dashing through the immediate area toward Mexico.

Connor smiled at the thought of it. Yes, everything was normal for this part of Arizona, for this time of the age. And everyone dashing about, always headed toward Mexico, it seemed.

New days came and went in these parts, but the news was always the same: tragedy, strife, mayhem, and murder — completely normal, mundane, almost boring for Tombstonians.

He was certain there was other news to report, but the newspaper company sold its product best when the news was at its most sensational.

Mister Gregorson's prize sow giving birth to ten piglets just wasn't newsworthy enough for it to be reported in the *Record-Epitaph*. Connor had to find that out directly from Mister Gregorson while earlier sharing a drink at the bar.

But anything from Geronimo's band or wild vicious bandits was accentuated, exaggerated, often to the extreme, and slapped onto the front page. Geronimo and bandits were still big news, and their characteristically devilish antics sold newspapers. So while the public, in these parts, had come to hold the old Apache chief up as something to be concerned about, but not overly so, newspaper editors all over the country held him up as critically vital to their continued endeavors. So it was also for bandits like the Brown Gang.

Maybe in the future, Connor thought, such sensationalist reporting by news organizations would eventually cease. Then he smiled as he realized that such reporting would most likely only get worse with the passage of time.

Finishing the edition, Connor folded the newspaper and placed it carefully back into the saddlebag with the others. Immediately, his mind drifted to his life on the ranch.

At times, it seemed, Connor was much like Tombstone. Life on the ranch was hard, but he loved it. And like the town of Tombstone, known as *the town too tough to die*, no matter how brutal the work and life on the ranch were, he was a tough man — *too tough to quit*.

It was good, though, to get into town now and then and away from the everyday stresses of ranch life. His wife, Sarah, would no doubt have supper waiting for him. Of course she would be expecting a suitable gift for allowing him to venture into town without her and the kids, to relax.

And it was a good thing for him he remembered all the little things Sarah needed but never asked for. She wasn't the kind of woman who ever asked for anything. She was that one in a million he had heard about.

The silver hairbrush would make her smile the most, Connor thought. And then he pictured her sitting in front of the large mirror in her cotton nightgown, stroking her hair with the soft-bristled brush, her eyes glowing as her softer blonde hair fell from those bristles back down over her even softer shoulders. But all of this would come after her tears of joy had dried, for without her knowledge, Connor had ordered two spectacular dresses for her through the Sears and Roebuck catalog on the trip into Tombstone the previous month.

He was amazed that things like dresses could be ordered and delivered so quickly from back east. With the advent of the railroad, it now took only days to get across the country. Sometimes he'd have to shake his head when he thought about how small the country had become. Now he could order dresses and have them delivered in only two weeks. Of course, it would be another two weeks before he would have the chance to pick them up. But the dresses were a remarkable eyeful.

He was absolutely positive that after she cut the twine and unwrapped the waxed paper and saw the dresses, the latest designs out of Chicago and New York, his wife's tears would flow for a great while. Then in a flash, her long, thin arms would wrap around his neck, her blue eyes would sparkle their joy, and those pink lips would press against his with love and gratitude.

Even after twelve years of marriage, Connor was still "in love" with his wife. Just the thought of her sent his heart fluttering wildly. He considered himself the luckiest man on earth, for Sarah was everything he imagined a good wife, friend, and lover could ever be.

His right hand slipped down off his thigh and patted a saddlebag filled with the other gifts for his bride, the jar of face cream, the lip rouge, the color for her eyelids, the multicolored ribbons for her hair, the new shoes.

In the opposite saddlebag he'd stored the sugar candy and the colored grease pencils for his eight-year-old daughter, Emma. She was the budding artist in the family, and when she wasn't in school or performing her chores around the ranch, she was seated at the table drawing the most wonderful pictures of ranch life Connor had ever seen. He could easily see the future for his daughter, displaying her art in exhibitions all over the United States.

Stuffed into the northwest-positioned scabbard next to his own Winchester rifle, the 1873 model, was a new Winchester 1873, 20-inch-barrel carbine, a birthday present for his nearly ten-year-old son, Benjamin. The lad's birthday was only a week away, but Connor knew that the second he spotted the wrapped rifle in the scabbard, he would have to let him have it right then and there.

Connor also accepted the fact that the sound of rifle fire would echo over the mountaintops surrounding the ranch for hours afterward. It was a good thing he'd purchased a full case of .44-40 cartridges during his visit to town the month before and was smart enough to hide them in among the other supplies in the wagon. Benjamin never saw them.

Connor smiled. He was the sneaky sort when he had to be. It was always a fun kind of sneaky, though.

He was prone to practical jokes when he thought he could get away with them. He had particular fun teasing his wife. In fact, he was already thinking how he might bring out each gift one at a time and string out her surprise for as long as he could.

Which gift would come out first and which one last vanished from his mind immediately as he topped the crest of a small hill and spotted the dark mass in the middle of the trail.

He heeled Tilly into a trot.

As he got closer to it, he saw that it was a dead horse.

He reined Tilly to a stop and slid down off her back and squatted down at the dead horse's head. He placed a hand on its neck. It appeared that it had died within the last four or five hours. Not more than six hours before, he guessed.

He studied the horse. It was not an old horse. In fact, it looked closer to being a colt. But its coat was matted. The horse had been nearly ridden to death and stripped of its saddle, then put out of its misery with a single bullet to the forehead.

And it was shod. The horse had given its all under the weight of a white man. He was certain of it.

He stood up and cast his eyes across the prairie in search of the man who obviously must be on foot and carrying a saddle.

He saw no one. Of course, within five or six hours someone could get a good distance away, but not very far in this heat and carrying a full rig on his back.

Since he had run across no one heading back toward Tombstone, he figured whoever it was might be headed south toward his ranch or one of the other spreads between here and his own.

He remounted Tilly and heeled her belly. She took off in a trot.

A half hour later, he came across another dead horse. As before, the horse looked run to death, missing the rig, and with a bullet hole in its head. But this horse was clearly on the trail that led only to his ranch. Someone was in a desperate rush to get to the ranch.

Concern and urgency revisited him. He heeled Tilly into a lope, knowing that his ranch was just over the next rise. Barring any other delay, he'd be home within thirty minutes.

Reaching the last hilltop, he caught sight of the descending sun on the western horizon to his right and the last rays of its reddening light slowly sweeping across the galvanized tin roof of his home and barn.

The gurgling in his stomach reminded him that he was growing hungry. But at that moment he had other concerns on his mind. Where were the two men and their saddles? Where were his wife and children?

When he was away, as he had been, the sinking sun usually beckoned Sarah to the doorway, her eyes expecting to see her husband approaching the ranch house from his restful day in town.

Although arriving earlier than normal, he was still surprised at not seeing Sarah at the door or the children playing in the yard.

In fact, he saw no movement at all surrounding the home. Then he noticed the gate to the corral was open and all the horses, fifty head, were missing. Also absent were strangers carrying saddles.

He heeled Tilly's belly again until the horse responded by lurching forward into a full gallop. Minutes later he reined back and halted the horse just in front of the opened front door to the cabin.

Dust swirled around him as he slipped down out of the saddle, and dashed in through the door.

"Sarah? Sarah darlin'?" he shouted.

He stopped in his tracks and his mouth dropped open in shock.

Laid out in a line in front of the dark, cold fireplace were the bodies of his family. Benjamin had a bullet hole straight through his young heart. Both of his girls were bloodied in their private parts, signs of violent violation. A single bullet hole through each heart apparently had finished them off.

Connor could not bring himself to go to them. Instead, he slumped to the floor, dropped his mournful eyes to the blood-soaked planking, and sat silently for two torturous hours, lost in the tearless blackness of a rising tempest of hate and rage.

CHAPTER 3

Connor's savaged young daughter was the last to be picked up off the floor and cradled in his arms as he carried her to the waiting grave.

Still no tears flowed from his eyes, no tears formed anywhere in his body. He wanted to cry. He should have cried. He would have allowed himself to cry, if he could have. But no tears found their way out of him. He reckoned there would never be any tears — ever. Of that he felt absolutely certain. He had no room for grief or sorrow. Only hate and revenge filled the space where all that should have been screaming out of him should be.

He gently laid Emma's body on the bottom of the clay grave, then went to his saddlebag and withdrew the gifts he had purchased in Tombstone for her. He laid them on her small chest, having performed the same ritual for Sarah and Benjamin, except he kept the new Winchester carbine, for he would have great need of it over the coming days.

He lifted the first shovelful of dirt over his young daughter and stopped. Something was wrong. He didn't know exactly what it was, but something was missing. He dropped the shovel and squatted over her grave, stared down onto his daughter's body, and thought about it.

After several minutes it dawned on him what was missing. "Where's Rebecca?" he muttered.

Rebecca was the cloth doll that Emma was never without, except perhaps during school, but she had even managed on several occasions to sneak Rebecca into school by tying the doll to her thigh with a bit of twine or ribbon meant for her hair. She was rarely seen without the doll, and Connor was going to make sure that Emma traveled into the great beyond clutching her "best friend," as she had considered her doll to be.

Connor searched the house thoroughly but was unable to find the doll. He then searched the yard wide and far. No Rebecca.

After a full half hour, without any luck, Connor resigned himself to the fact that somehow Rebecca was gone forever. During the assault, the doll had probably been tossed somewhere he would never think to look. Perhaps Emma had hidden Rebecca away so that she might be spared the horror of the attack. Emma was like that.

He finally gave up the search and returned to the graves where, with rugged resolve and deep sadness, he began shoveling the soil back into all the pits, covering his daughter's beautiful face first and then his son's. Lastly, his wife's sweet face disappeared under the shovelfuls of clay and granite pebbles.

Three fresh mounds of dirt dotted the land, each outlined by large rocks. A flat piece of sandstone marked the head of each grave. Scribbled on each marker was the heartbreaking information for its occupant.

Connor stood up when he'd finished wearing what could barely pass as a smile on his lips.

The graves, located at the base of the huge south-facing sandstone cliff, which rose two hundred feet immediately behind the home, were perfectly placed.

Sarah had enjoyed this particular spot, which she often could be found sitting in, relishing the shade between the house and the cliff, while reading or knitting.

Now she and the children would forever enjoy the shade of the cliff.

Connor wiped a shirtsleeve across his wet brow. Normally, it would be time to speak a few words over the dearly departed and his mind searched for just such words, but there were none to be found. His head was as empty as his heart was full of overwhelming hatred.

He could ask God to watch over them, but the thought of a just god allowing this to happen to his beloved family rendered any wish for assistance pointless. He could see no purpose in talking to such a spiteful, heartless being.

He turned and, for a moment, studied the dying sun sinking into the western horizon.

He was suddenly struck with exhaustion.

The burials had taken him all day. Digging one grave in the hard clay soil of the ranch was tough enough for any man. Connor had dug three.

Now that his gruesome task had been completed, he staggered back to his house.

Stepping up onto the ramada, he set the tools against the exterior wall and pushed the door open. A rancid odor engulfed him, and he saw the pools of coagulated blood on the floor. He stared at them for several moments with an empty stare before finally gritting his teeth in both anger and fatigue. One more ghastly chore to perform before the house would come anywhere close to being normal.

He grabbed a wooden bucket from the counter, staggered out to the pump, and filled it. Retrieving the bar of lye soap from the pail that hung from the pump handle, and a hard-bristled brush, he staggered back toward the house.

Moments later, he was on his knees scrubbing and mopping up the blood spots with an old woolen shirt, now used as a rag. He scrubbed the area until the wood was scarred white, but it was no use. In his mind's eye those terrible stains were still there. And they would always be there as a chilling reminder of his failure as both a husband and a father.

He looked up at the ceiling of the cabin and screamed his rage. Then he saw the spatters of blood all the way up on the ceiling boards.

He slammed the brush to the floor. It bounced away from him toward the wooden sink. He watched it bound upward and back down and skid across the floor and smack into the dark-stained pine cabinet.

His eye caught something. He immediately crawled over to it and plucked it off the small nail that normally held oven gloves. Even in the dim light of the lantern on the table, he could see it was a torn piece of tanned leather with the unmistakable markings of the Apache stained onto it.

He guessed that the brave had brushed up against the nail and the leather had ripped. His mind invented the struggle in which his wife battled with the Indian. He saw the leather shirt or pants catching on the nail and ripping.

An all-consuming abhorrence came over him, and the heavy press of revenge quashed any bit of remaining reason there might have been in his rapidly narrowing mind. He could now put a face to the demon, in this case a band of demons — vile creatures all, absent any compassion or appreciation for human life; vicious and despicable monsters who only minimally displayed the outward appearance of being human; who were, in reality, animals without a heart or a soul…or any fragment of divine consciousness. Apaches.

He hurled the bucket against the wall, shattering it and splashing the bloodied water back onto the floor. He gritted his teeth once more and his eyes filled with something indescribable but far beyond hate. He closed them tightly and grimaced until he could no longer contain his hurt and shame.

Finally he reared his head back like a baying coyote and shouted curses into the air — curses against everything he had ever believed in, curses which had their creation either somewhere in the black abyss that was now his soul or in the decaying guts of Hell itself. An odious manifestation surged through him and out into the night air in one loud and hateful roar.

After his rage had subsided and his shouting had quieted, he sat staring intently at that small, telling piece of animal skin. His mind began to discover the answers to the questions which had formed in his brain from the beginning of the nightmare. The savage murders had been perpetrated by a raiding party of Apaches; it was beginning to make sense.

His mind reeled as he recalled scanning the article from the pages of the *Record-Epitaph* citing the breakout of Geronimo and his band of followers from the San Carlos Reservation a few weeks earlier. The news story reported the belief of army officials that they might be heading south toward their favorite area, the northern Sonoran Desert mountains near Cananea, Mexico.

If the story was true, it was logical to expect them to travel quite near his ranch. In fact, it was extremely likely for them to do so. However, after their nearly 150-mile trek, made unbearably arduous, no doubt, by the hot pursuit of the U.S. Army, their horses were most likely worn out or dead. They had probably eaten most of them by the time they had come upon the Double Bar T. As a result, they would sorely need fresh mounts to complete the last fifty-five miles of their escape from the American pursuers. They would need supplies as well before launching themselves into the mountains of Mexico.

They must have raided his ranch and, finding his family alone and vulnerable, exacted a revenge against the helpless white family — *his* family — the family unfortunately in their treacherous path.

But what of the two shod horses? Where had the Apache gotten those horses? He challenged his mind to explain it. In answer to the challenge, it created a vision of the Apaches stealing the horses from a white family — perhaps the family in Silver City they had murdered. The sense of it was now confirmed.

They obviously did this dastardly deed with little or no regard for the ages of their victims. Surely, one must be possessed of a wicked heart to harm children. Connor was determined now to put bullets through each one of their scornful hearts until not one Apache lived.

A twinge of regret stabbed at his heart as he realized that he might have become the very demon he had always feared. But he dismissed the regret quickly. Regret required that there first be compassion and understanding, and his heart and mind had little room for anything that was not hate and rage.

It didn't matter to Connor how many he might face. He was going to track them down and kill every redskin he found. Man, woman, or child, it didn't matter. He would adopt their principles, their methods, their means. He would become just like them. He would exact a dreadful vengeance upon those godless creatures. He would avenge his family if it was the last thing he ever did on this earth, staining the dirt forever red with savage blood.

A smothering rage returned — a rage that invaded every cell and fiber of his being and he screamed again in existential pain.

At that moment, the last vestige of the conscience that had once existed within him vanished in the reverberation of his agonized scream.

He detested himself for leaving his family alone and vulnerable while he selfishly relaxed in Tombstone on that fateful day. Had he been more thoughtful and considerate, less selfish, he would have hitched up the wagon and his entire family would have been in town with him, not dying torturous and tragic deaths at home.

A blackness overtook his mind, creating a hideous beast that loathed *everyone* and *everything*.

A single word filled his brain: *extermination*.

He set a new goal for himself, the utter and complete extermination of his foe from the face of the earth.

Connor held the thought of extermination in his mind and let it fill each and every cell of his being with its terrible blackness until he finally collapsed onto the floor in near unconsciousness. The exhaustion and stress of his hate had finally taken its toll. He rolled over onto his back against the hard planking of the floor and fell fast asleep.

CHAPTER 4

Sitting at the table, bathed in the dim light of a single kerosene lamp, he finished wiping down the tools in support of his new purpose — two Winchester rifles, a Colt Peacemaker, and a thousand rounds of interchangeable .44-40 ammunition.

He considered who and what he needed to exact his vengeance upon the Apache. Was there room in his hate-filled heart for a demon — a demon he needed to fulfill his murderous quest? No, he reasoned. He didn't require any assistance from any other demon. For what had already manifested within him, and was growing in power and purpose, was much worse. The black-hearted thing that had already found a place in his heart was going to make any demon look like a lamb. The thing in him was pure hate. Its only desire was vengeance. Its only purpose was to destroy those who had murdered his family.

He walked to the door and cast his eyes eastward. The hint of morning to come found him welcoming neither the day nor the night. It was all the same to him. All he could see was the blackness of his own mind.

By the time the pink hue emerged on the eastern horizon, Connor Beckett stood next to Tilly with a stabbing, immutable purpose. He calmly finished packing his saddlebags with everything he could carry and walked up the two steps of the ramada and into the cabin.

He walked directly to the mantel, removed the small family portrait he'd had taken some months before at Tombstone's C. S. Fly's photo studio and stared at it for several seconds. Then he nonchalantly struck the frame against the stone mantel, shattering the glass, and stuffed the portrait under his leather vest and into the breast pocket of his shirt. He moved to the table, picked up the can of kerosene, and splashed it onto the floors and walls of the wood structure.

Backing up toward the door, he poured what was left of the kerosene on the floor in a trail until he stood on the ramada and dropped the can at his feet. His eyes were fixed and hard. He felt no sadness, no hurt, no regret. He felt no emotions at all. Emotions were for someone alive — something someone with a flicker of hope still living inside them grasps onto for support, or reason, or purpose — something for someone with a future.

His mind accommodated only a terrible resolve — a horrifying and oppressing resolve. He could see nothing past the existing day for himself. The black thing within him prevented him from seeing anything beyond the mist of the hatred clouding his brain. He affirmed his rebirth to that new purpose: vengeance. And to the extinction of an entire species of animal known as the Apache.

Holding fast to that new determination, he struck the match against the ramada's support pole and dropped it toward his feet and into the rivulet of kerosene and then watched the snake-like track of fire quickly work its way in through the door until the explosion of violent flames lit up the interior of the wood-frame house.

He serenely stepped off the ramada and backed into the yard, his eyes fixed on the growing inferno. He took Tilly's reins in his hand as he watched the fire reach up to the roof in searing licks. Emotion remained absent. There was no hint of life in the icy dark orbs that were his eyes.

At his feet lay the tied, unread bundle of the *Record-Epitaph*. He looked down at it, then picked it up. He stared at it for a moment and then hurled it into the flames. He had no more use for knowledge and wisdom — no more use for knowing or caring what transpired in the world around him. His world had shriveled to only what now existed within his hate-filled mind.

The light of the rising flames collided with the dim hint of morning hues, as they both reflected off the sandstone cliff face. By the time the rays of sunrise reached the timbers of the house, they would be only cinders. The sun would never again rise upon that wicked place. No one would ever live there again. No one would ever suffer there again. It was no longer a home. It had ceased being a home the moment Connor's family was murdered. It was now just an accursed construct of wood, stone, and stucco. Soon, being purified by the consuming flames, it would be reduced to only a sorrowful and scathing memory.

Although the brightness of those flames projected their dancing images against the surrounding cliff, light had ceased any existence within him, and he could not see how any amount of illumination could ever dispel the ominous darkness that dwelt now within his tormented, burnt, and blackened soul.

Connor mounted Tilly, reined her neck to the south, and, picking up the tracks of his stolen horses, set out on his new life as hunter of the Apache, never once glancing back at his former life now engulfed in flames.

Gerald Thompson slammed the journal shut and stood up.

"Whew! The intensity of this has given me the shakes. May I join you at the fire, sir?"

Geronimo motioned for Thompson to come sit beside him.

"Is it the story you wanted, Mister Thompson?"

The reporter staggered toward Geronimo on unsteady legs.

"It is, sir. But I must say, it's almost too much to bear all at once. The intensity of his thoughts are stifling. I found my breath bein' snatched from me for a moment. I thought my heart was gonna seize up."

"Is it exciting enough for your readers in Kansas City?"

"That and beyond, sir. Certainly I have heard of such rage, and fear, and loathing, and sorrow. But I never believed it was anything but an author's imagination. This, though, I can feel it. I can feel it in his words. I believe if I close my eyes, I can actually see what he's goin' through."

"Have you ever lost anyone close to you, Mister Thompson?"

"No, sir. I'm not married. I'm an only child and my parents are still alive and living in St. Louis, where I'm originally from. No, sir, I've never lost anyone close to me. I can only imagine what Mister Beckett must have gone through."

"It is a terrible thing to bury your family while you remain among the living."

"Is that how you felt, Geronimo? Is that the kinda pain you experienced?"

"Connor Beckett and I are brothers in the pain of loss, Mister Thompson."

"My Lord, I can't imagine goin' home to my family murdered so gruesomely."

"Loss is a tragic thing. It is a fire that does not die out."

"Do you still think about your murdered family, Geronimo?"

"Every day, Mister Thompson. Every day I see my wife smile and my three children playing.

Sometimes I feel lost in those memories. And lost is something only to be found through misfortune."

"Indeed it is, sir. What were their names?"

"It is not polite to talk of the dead, Mister Thompson. I know their names. That is all I will say."

"Certainly, sir. Certainly. I didn't mean to be rude."

"Even now, I see them so very clearly. I should cry some more for them, but I'm afraid I have no more tears for anything or anyone."

"Would I be rude to ask where they died?"

"Janos, Mexico. They were killed by Mexicans who had no…"

Geronimo fell silent and bowed his head and remained still for almost two minutes before he lifted his head and spoke, his eyes fixed on the flames of his fire.

"It is not good that I should say bad things about anyone anymore. I am not liked among my own people. Many say that I should be hanged for all the misery I have caused. So how can I speak evil of others?"

"I understand, sir. But I don't know what I would do different if I found my family murdered."

"On that night, I did not know what to do either. Rage and hate had not yet found their path to my heart. I stood by the river most of the night thinking of my family. Finally, Mangas Coloradas ordered us to walk home. It was a long and dark night. I walked last in the line, far behind. I only heard the voices of the others quietly talking ahead of me. I was alone. I had never felt so alone as that night, on that long walk. Hours before I was a son, a husband, and a father. In only a moment, I became nothing but alone."

"I am so sorry for that, Geronimo. I can see why you feel close to Connor Beckett. I reckon you two could tell your stories and there would be no difference between them."

"Go read more, Mister Thompson. I want to think about my family now. I want to become lost again in those memories."

"Yes, sir. I leave you to your sweet memories."

The reporter arose and walked to the ramada. Sitting back down on the chair, he stared at Geronimo, who had, once again, discovered a remembrance up in the heavens. He smiled sadly as he opened the journal.

CHAPTER 5

The trail left by fifty close-ordered horses and their companions was an easy trail to follow, like following the trail left by a U.S. Cavalry brigade. It was well defined and required no special skill. The tracks of the shod and unshod horses didn't appear to be more than two days old. It was their trail, the ones that had murdered his family. Connor was certain of it. He reinforced his will to track them into Hell itself and dine on their flesh for breakfast. And he would smile doing it.

A chill shot down his spine when he suddenly realized that he must have been riding home from Tombstone at the same time his family was being tortured and murdered. That would explain the intense feeling of urgency that had swept over him in Tombstone. It must have been their souls calling out to him for help. That also might explain why the urgency had ceased so abruptly, at the moment when their souls left their bodies.

A surge of white-hot hatred shot through him like a searing spike.

He looked skyward and screamed.

Once he'd calmed down, he returned to thoughts of vengeance. Maybe Tombstone was too tough to die, but the Apache weren't. He was going to make sure of that, and he was going to make certain each one of them would become personally acquainted with the terrors, the horrors, and the exquisite pain of death he imagined his family experiencing.

A guilty thought pierced him sharply. If he had left for home only a few hours earlier he might have been able to save them. Then another thought bumped that one aside as he realized that instead of saving them, he might have died alongside them.

That might have been a comforting thought to the old Connor Beckett, but with the stronger stirs of murder and revenge filling his wounded mind, he felt glad to have been spared. For now, he had both the means and the motive to exact a reckoning on the savages that few had had before him. And he vowed to make their demise as torturous as humanly possible, though his own humanity had been left behind, consumed by the flames.

The sun beat down upon him mercilessly as he reined Tilly to a stop. He guessed it was near to 100 degrees already, and from the looks of the sun's position in the sky, he figured it was about ten in the morning. It was sure to get much hotter before this day ended.

He pulled his canteen off the horn and tugged the cork free. With one hand on the pommel of the saddle, he braced himself, leaned his head back, and took three long swallows. Having enough water was going to be an issue soon, but he recalled a spring of clear, cool water about five miles ahead. With luck and only fifty-five miles to go until he hit the Mexican border, he figured to be staring down on those murdering Apache within two days, from a ridge he knew well.

When the firing started, he would have the initial advantage of twenty-nine combined rounds in both rifles. He would save his revolver for close-order fighting, which was sure to follow once the savages knew they faced only a solitary man on the nearby ridge, albeit a man who rarely missed what he aimed at. They would attack quickly, sacrificing a few good braves if need be for a quick kill of the White-Eye dogging them.

Another, better plan came to him. The newspaper article had indicated that Geronimo had only about thirty to forty fierce fighting braves with him. The rest of the tribe's contingent was made up of women, children, and the elderly. Connor believed that if he picked off the braves before anyone else in a "shoot and run" tactic, as he had done during the war back in '65, he could even the odds a little. He was a crack shot with a single-shot, muzzle-loaded Enfield. With this modern repeating Winchester, he expected to drop a bunch of them before they knew what hit them.

He knew the terrain well and figured to gallop away from the initial fight and set himself up on a rise of ground a half mile or so farther away and wait for the savages to continue their attack, drawing them closer and into a sizzling death zone somewhere less than two hundred yards from him.

During the war in the thick forests of Tennessee, his lead officer called it a "staggered redeployment." In reality, it was a carefully designed strategy designed to kill off as many of the enemy as were foolish enough to think *they* were the pursuers.

There were plenty of rises in the terrain heading back toward the ranch that presented him with an excellent firing position. The Apache were fiercely bred fighters, and he was hoping they wouldn't give up too easily upon seeing many of their braves fall to Connor's hail of precision gunfire. If they showed any sign of stalling or quitting, he'd goad them, if he could, into continuing their attack. The more he brought toward him, the more would fall, to die on the desert floor and perish as rotting lumps under mounting sand — fitting end markers for their despicable lives.

If they decided the risk was too great and returned to their camp, ignoring his taunts, then he would just track them down again and duplicate his bloody campaign. Eventually, after successfully repeating this maneuver enough times, he hoped to take all the braves down. The women, the children, the old, and the infirm would then be easy kills. And he would force Geronimo to watch it all before putting him onto his own personal path to Hell.

The sun crawled torturously slowly across the sky, unyielding in its attempt to deter the lone rider from his dark quest, but Connor refused to surrender. A great avenging task had been set before him and he would not allow anything to sway him from such a solemn duty. Besides, he reasoned, if he suffered from the heat, surely those he pursued suffered equally. After all, Pastor Ringdahl had once sermoned that the sun shone equally upon the just and the unjust alike. Even without the sun, the mean desert was a great equalizer. Yes, he thought, even for someone born and raised in its midst such as he.

Having been born near Santa Fe, in the soon-to-be New Mexico Territory, he had been a part of the desert, or it had been a part of him, for forty years. He understood the desert. At least as much as the desert allowed anyone to understand it.

———❧———

The tracks had remained unmistakably true. Keeping an eye more on the unshod hoof marks — signs of the Apache — he continued his deadly pursuit until he came to a slight rise in the ground.

By the position of the sun, he guessed it was approaching three o'clock. After five hot and exhausting miles under the midday sun, he was looking forward to the cool spring water which lay about two hundred yards past the rise ahead in a small, rocky mound in the desert. It was a well-known watering hole, often visited by anyone passing through the area.

Being the naturally cautious type, he slipped down off his horse, pulled his full-length rifle from its scabbard, and dropped to his belly just before the peak of the rise. He removed his hat and crawled the rest of the way on his belly, stopping once to pick up a desert scorpion by the tail and toss it away. He had no special reason for allowing the scorpion to live. It was just that he had more meaningful murder on his mind.

It was a good thing that he had decided to crawl on his belly into position, for reaching the summit and peering over it and down to the spring, he spotted three Indian braves nonchalantly watering their horses.

He'd had no idea before this moment how easy this was going to be. These three braves were going to be the first test of his new resolve and purpose — the madness of his revenge.

He carefully depressed the rear-sight elevator release and slid it forward to the two-hundred-yard mark, then placed it against his cheek and sighted down the rifle.

The Indians stood next to their horses, calmly waiting for their mounts to finish drinking from the pool.

Connor wished for no prolonged fight with these savages. Three young bucks were too many to entertain any thoughts of torture or game-playing. This would have to be a simple cool case of icy revenge. Before pulling the trigger, he took the time to study them and their apparel carefully. Something was wrong; they weren't Apache. He then recognized their markings as Navajo.

It was widely known that Geronimo was of the Bedonkohe Apache, a part of the Mescalero-Chiricahua Apache clan. He was not often seen in the company of the Navajo. In fact, throughout the area, it was commonly rumored that Geronimo had fought against the Navajo on many occasions and that they were essentially his enemies. But then Connor recalled the age-old proverb: *The enemy of my enemy is my friend*. Perhaps in his war against the White-Eye, Geronimo had set aside the differences between the tribes and developed a working relationship, concentrating more on their larger and more dangerous foe, the invading white men.

Whether or not they were allied with the murderous Geronimo mattered little to him. Navajo or Apache or Cheyenne or whatever, Connor saw them all as animals deserving equal disdain.

He centered the hub of the rifle's front sight on the head of one of the Navajo braves. "This is for Sarah," he announced to himself.

Then he thought, being so close to the ranch, might these savages have been directly involved with his family's murders? The one currently in his sights, could he be one of those who had violated his wife so viciously, or might he be the one who had put the bullet through her heart? Perhaps he was one of them who had violated his young daughter. Or perhaps these men had nothing to do with what had happened back on the ranch. He had no way of knowing, of course, but he realized that he didn't care. They were savages and they were going to die.

Besides, at the end of all his thinking lay one immutable fact. There could be only one solution to satisfy him in the red fog of his bloodlust. He squeezed the trigger, and the rifle cartridge detonated. A second later, the Navajo's head disintegrated into a bloody mass of scattering skull matter.

As fast as a lightning bolt, he chambered another round. "For Benjamin," he muttered as he aimed and fired. Another Navajo brave, trying to mount his horse, would not return to his tribe that evening after the .44 caliber bullet ripped through his back, piercing his heart.

The third brave successfully swung up onto the back of his horse. He reined it hard to the right in an effort to head it in the opposite direction and put as much distance between him and the skilled assassin as quickly as he was able.

His effort was too little, too late.

His horse was fast, but not faster than a bullet. "For my sweet Emma," Connor said through gritted teeth. His third shot struck the brave square in the spine in the center of his back. He was dead before he hit the ground.

He thought about taking their scalps, but quickly dismissed the thought. He was not out for trophies. He was out purely for the sake of vengeance.

A few minutes later, Connor rode past the last bloodied body, still following the tracks made by his stolen horses. He didn't look at the body as he passed.

That lack of scrutiny was not out of mercy for the dead. The black pits that were now his eyes held no merciful consideration; they were already searching for the next savages to kill.

At that moment, if he'd been able, he would have scorched the earth itself to be rid of his pursued prey, even if that meant that he would go up in the same flames. He didn't plan on living through this event anyway, so what could it matter?

All earlier thoughts of torturing his prey before dispatching them into the next world vanished. Through a brief interlude of calmer thinking, he reasoned that any time spent on the delicious pursuit of torture would only delay him from his more meaningful goal — the complete annihilation of the Apaches.

As for the savages he hunted, every filthy one of them he came across would be ended in the same manner as the last three. As far as Connor Beckett was concerned, they were already dead. They just needed the impact of his bullet to complete their departure.

His only regret was having brought a paltry thousand rounds of ammunition with him. He wished he had ten times as many.

It didn't matter to him whether or not those three dead Indians had been at the ranch. His intent was to clean all savages off the face of the planet — at least off of his little piece of it.

Emotion, unable to be contained any longer, expressed itself in the form of tears spilling over and leaving muddy streaks down his dust-covered cheeks. These were tears born not of fear or sorrow, but of a devouring hate deep within him — a hate only a tortured few would ever know.

The transformation of his soul was now complete. Its blackness tolerated no thought of light, let alone the illuminated presence of any light itself. He had by then so dedicated himself to his dark, murderous mission that the only thing that could stop him was its completion or a bullet with his name on it. Until then, the purpose of his deadly mission was clear and unobstructed.

The cool water of the spring had flowed down his gullet with ease and appreciation. He was now feeling refreshed and able to continue his pursuit.

While the blistering sun wore him down relentlessly, cooking his skin and frying his brain, the revulsion he felt for every red-skinned *animal*, as all Indians had become to him, revitalized him and restored his drive. With both his canteens full of fresh water, and Tilly refreshed and rested, they plodded onward across the harsh southwest sands, following the many tracks lying undisturbed ahead of them.

The tracks were getting fresher by the hour. He was gaining on them. Considering that he traveled alone, unlike Geronimo, who had to move an entire band including women, children, and old people, he guessed he was perhaps only twelve to fifteen hours behind them.

It was unlikely that anyone would willingly rush headlong across this desert. Not through this sweltering, indefensible heat. It was simply far too much for anyone or anything to do that without a mighty good reason. Of course, Connor reasoned, pursuing wicked criminals or running for your life would be reason enough for such a crossing, but even a then it wasn't wise to do so hastily.

It was more likely that the Apache would maintain a slow and steady pace. It was the only reasonable course of action for anyone under the diabolical press of the desert heat. Connor included himself in that assessment.

He intended to follow them steadily, biding his time. It would do him no good to kill Tilly in trying to make up the distance in one burst. No, he thought, his pursuit would be steady, sure and unyielding. His purpose remained fixed in his brain. No unnecessary deviation was acceptable to him. He was on the vicious and unforgiving task of vengeance. Nothing would get him to alter that purpose. Nothing and no one.

There was more water ahead, but it was another twelve miles away, through the worst of the desert to come. Perhaps Geronimo knew of water sources unknown to the White-Eye; it mattered little to him. As long as he followed them in the manner he was taking, he would eventually have access to everything they had. So long as no windstorms arose and blew away the tracks, he would keep his easy pace.

The last thing he wanted was to kill his horse trying to press too hard. If that happened, he would soon follow Tilly and his family into the afterlife, and he wasn't ready to die just yet. Not until he had slaughtered every savage in the area. Maybe then, afterward, he would put the final bullet into his own head. Why not? There was no life for him after his black deeds were done. In fact, the more he thought about it, the more eager he was to join his family.

But first there was much slaughtering to be done. Before that, though, was the night. And it would be upon him within the next couple of hours.

Here, in the lands immediately east of the northern Sonoran Desert, high on the Escalante, on a moonless night, everyone had to yield to the night. Even if he rushed to catch up to them just before nightfall, it would be much too dark to launch any kind of effective assault on them. Night fighting was held to a minimum for good reason.

The moonless night to come would make it nearly impossible for him to see his own hand before his face, even in the starlight. It was impossible to travel over this terrain in the dark; the desert floor was strewn with loose rocks and varmint holes that tended to break horses' legs, not to mention that it was impossible to know in which direction you were going in the blindness of the night.

Timing was as important to him as anything. He had to catch them at the right moment in order to be fully effective. It would be best if they were out in the open, tired, thirsty, their movement hindered by both the old and the very young. He tried to consider all aspects of his chase thoroughly. Mistakes out here, exposed as he would be, could easily result in his own death long before he was able to effect his full retribution on those he pursued so tenaciously.

CHAPTER 6

Connor stopped and dismounted in the middle of a flat, featureless terrain. The air was so still and stifling that he found it difficult to draw a full breath. From the sun's position, it was near to seven o'clock — the still glaring sun maintaining most of the day's heat.

He pulled his hat off his head, rammed his fist into the top of it, rounding it out into a bowl; he filled it halfway with water from his canteen and held it under Tilly's muzzle. She sucked it dry and wanted more, but Connor had given her what he could spare.

Following a soft stroke along her neck, his forehead laid up against hers, he whispered through cracked and dried lips, "We're doing good, girl. But we have far to go."

The horse whinnied loudly, as if to agree with his assessment. Or perhaps she was asking for a reprieve from the deadly pursuit for her own sake. She would have to understand his need to pursue those ahead of them, though. She would have to, or he would force her to. Nothing was going to stop him.

Leading Tilly with the reins in his swollen and sun-reddened hand, he walked ahead of her, following the tracks across the even drier desert floor, heading for a distant range of high hills directly ahead — the Huachuca Mountains.

The longer he traveled alongside the tracks, the more certain he was of the Apaches' involvement.

The unshod hoof marks left by the Apache ponies blended in with his shod horses. It was as if they were purposefully trying to hide their presence amid his stolen herd. Connor was an experienced tracker, a specialty he'd developed during the Civil War, and it was evident to him that some unshod ponies ran among the pack while others came up from behind.

They were difficult to spot, but every once in a while he noted an unshod hoof mark on top of the others. A few Apache, it seemed, were tasked with staying back from the main herd, possibly acting as rear guards.

Connor stopped, dismounted, and knelt down next to one particular set of tracks. They were fresher, and they overlaid the others. These had been made only within the last six hours or so, while the underlying tracks, the tracks he had been following, had been made much earlier, nearly twice that long ago.

Where had they come from? He hadn't seen them before now. It was either the black magic of the Apache, or the rear guard had straggled that far behind and had come into the main tracks from another direction. Maybe he'd missed them coming into the main tracks a while ago. But why were they such a great distance behind?

Under the relentless sun, disturbed sandy loam dried out quickly. To an experienced tracker like Connor, the timing was a critical clue and his conclusion was simple. The main body of the herd was still many hours ahead of him, but the rear guard was only six or so hours ahead. Maybe less, if they had stopped for the night as well.

He concluded that he was either gaining quickly on them, or someone else was in pursuit of the herd. Perhaps, he thought, the others might be connected to the Navajo he had killed earlier. Perhaps they were tracking the herd for reasons of their own.

Connor mounted his horse, drank a few swallows from his canteen, then heeled Tilly forward as the awful memories of his family continued playing in his mind. He tried to keep them playing over and over; it helped him keep the hatred strong in his heart even while the sun tried its best to bake acquiescence into him.

Often, even the mightiest anger, carried in the hearts of very violent people, would lose its zest out here under the blazing heat of the sun. Its unbearable assault on an exposed man tired him without end, sapping nearly every drop of energy from him. It was hard for anyone traveling through these unrelenting elements to keep any other thought but that of the most basic and primal survival considerations as the desert did its best to kill you.

Connor fought the sun's attack. With the picture of his murdered family in his mind, his hate grew stronger and became more powerful than the desert's wish to bury him. Those visions kept him going.

Another blistering hour passed before he finally reined Tilly to a stop and slid down from the saddle to stretch his legs.

Despite the savages initially having almost a forty-eight-hour head start on him, his steady pursuit and quicker pace had him closing upon them quickly. With any luck at all, he figured he'd have a clear shot at the braves sometime late the next afternoon. That was, of course, unless their scouts spotted him first.

With the trail clearly leading him directly toward the mountains, he knew that once they were in the higher elevations, the scouts would have a full field of vision back toward him. If they did indeed spot him, he faced a multitude of poor conclusions for himself, but that was no reason to turn back and stop this pursuit. He'd never figured to live past the end of his mission anyway. The best he could hope for was to live long enough to complete his task.

He moved slowly, knowing that any cloud of dust would be easily and most likely quickly spotted by Geronimo's lookouts. If he was spotted, he would lose his advantage over them. Surprise was essential. He intended to make the announcement of his arrival a loud one, a devastating one — a profound and deadly one. The rifle fire and the dropping bodies would be warning enough that a man possessed by a terrible evil was on their trail. With that thought, a sickened smile stretched his lips.

The path the Apache were taking was a logical one. Geronimo knew this whole area like the back of his hand, and he was certainly aware of the location of Fort Huachuca near the entrance to a southward leading canyon that passed eventually very near to the Town of Bisbee, approximately 30 miles southeast.

With the U.S. Army close by and no doubt on high alert for Geronimo by now, Connor saw his pursuit as a race against the army as to who would be the first to kill the savages, so feared and yet, ironically, revered throughout these parts of the new Arizona Territory.

It was certain to be no easy task, though. It had been reported before that Geronimo had once stated that the best place to hide from an enemy was right under their noses. And Connor wouldn't put it past the clever tribal chief to lead his people quietly past the fort and up into the canyon, where he knew he could best protect them — right past those searching eyes — those searching, blind eyes that would never expect Geronimo to do such a thing.

From high in the Huachucas, his keen-eyed scouts would see anyone in pursuit of them long before those in pursuit would see the huddled band.

An hour later, very near the mountains, Connor saw a sudden change in the tracks. Sliding down from the saddle, he squatted near the break in the trail.

A quick glance startled him. The trail separated, with the shod horses veering left as if to go around the mountains while the unshod ponies continued directly toward the range.

Connor scratched at his whiskers. *What could be the purpose of doing this?* he thought. He knew these mountains, too. They weren't hazardously steep. The horses would have little or no trouble negotiating the slope toward the upper grazing areas. He had been there many times before. The grasslands were gently sloping, especially near the streams falling from the summit toward the desert floor.

So why did Geronimo split the herd? Connor asked himself the question over and over, with no answer forthcoming.

To compound the issue, assuming that the Apache were most likely eating the horses along the way, it made even less sense to separate the food source from the tribe.

Once the herd was separated, it would be no easy task to bring them back together. Except for the main canyon, the Huachucas were mostly a wide expanse of hills and valleys offering limited routes of passage. Once committed to going around the area, it would not be simple to change.

Separated from an easy food source, the Apache would have to rely on what they could snare or kill up on the mountain pastures. As far as Connor knew, that meant an occasional stray cow, but more commonly small rodents and fowl, not necessarily a savory or filling meal for nearly forty people.

Without supplies to hold them very long, Connor believed Geronimo would sooner or later have to lead his starving band quietly past the small new mining town of Bisbee in some fashion, most likely by climbing up around the town at night — an extremely dangerous move considering the vulnerability of both the very young and the very old.

Along the way he would have to secure some badly needed supplies for the women and children of his band from the miners and settlers living near the town. So as not to expose their whereabouts, he would have to send out several braves on silent and deadly raiding parties, leaving no witnesses.

If Connor could exercise patience, he might be able to kill the small raiding party of braves. Without the supplies brought back from his raiders, Geronimo would then have to rush through the area, pushing both the young and old to their maximum limits. Perhaps they might die from sheer exhaustion during the arduously long trek through the passes of the Huachucas.

Of course, once safely past Bisbee, he expected Geronimo to break out of the area in a mad dash for the area surrounding Cananea, a small border settlement. Cananea was also well known to Geronimo and it seemed, to Connor, the most logical destination for an escaping horde of Indians trying to elude the persistent pursuit of the U.S. Army. Of course, Geronimo had hidden from them so successfully, so far, that Connor didn't see Cananea as a problem for the crafty chief to scoot past the army scouts.

From there, Geronimo would make a burst up into the northern Sierra Madre and then south, deep into the Sonoran Desert. If he was successful in getting that far, he would be lost to all for quite a while. Even the army scouts from both countries would be hard pressed to find his people in the wide expanse of that vast desert area.

If Geronimo did manage to get his people that far, even Connor's pursuit would become nearly impossible, but unlike the U.S. Army, Connor had already picked up the trail of the desperately driven Apache.

It was certain, in *his* mind at least, that with the expected breakout, he would at best have a devil of a time keeping up with them. In fact, he well expected to be introduced to several other devils throughout the Sonoran highlands, namely the unscrupulous and terrifying banditos that made their home all through the area. The Mexican bandits hated Geronimo, but they hated the gringos more. Any white man caught intruding across the border could expect a long, torturous ordeal and a slow, painful death.

Considering what he faced, he finally muttered aloud, "I'd rather battle against the devils I know than the devils I don't know. But I'll be happy to slaughter both."

Hampered by his need to make a decision about which trail to follow, he fell behind his scheduled arrival into the foothills of the Huachucas. They were at least another hour's ride away and the sun was already diving headlong into the western horizon. Within several minutes, the desert would fall into a deep darkness and things would change drastically for the lone rider.

A scorching landscape during the daylight hours, the desert could get mighty chilly after sundown, and out here on the scrubland where he now found himself, a fire surely made it both tolerable and safer. The night animals had learned to stay away from fire — reptiles like the western diamondback rattlesnake and the Gila monster, insects like the scorpions and assorted spiders, and large animals like the wolf and coyote, they knew to stay away from the light and heat of man.

Nighttime was their time to hunt and feed, but even a modest fire kept them comfortably away so that one exhausted from the blistering heat of the day might catch a wink or two of sleep during the night without worrying about being attacked. But out here, fully exposed as he was, Connor would not be allowed the comfort of a warming fire for fear of giving away his location. Without the aid of such a fire, he accepted the fact that he would have to keep his eyes keenly peeled in between winks of sleep.

The lack of food had been an issue from the very start of his campaign. One of his saddlebags was full of jerky. That would be his meal morning, noon, and night for a while and he had already resigned himself to that fact. He had water enough to sustain him through the night, but the lack of a fire was going to press him hard to get through to morning with any comfort. He had no choice, however; without sunlight, he was going nowhere.

He lifted a short length of rope from the saddlebag and hobbled Tilly to prevent her from wandering off during the night.

Finding the reason for Geronimo splitting up the herd would have to wait until sunup. For now he could only sit in the dark, chewing on a shard of jerky and regretting the indecision that had put him in the center of the desert's black heart.

What had prevented him from choosing one trail or the other? He tried to reason through it. *Why had the decision been so hard for him to make*? Such indecisiveness was uncharacteristic of him, for Connor Beckett was a decisive man. He knew that about himself. And once he made a decision, he wasted little time considering any alternative options.

He continued trying to reason it out. At the same time, he tried getting into the mind of Geronimo to understand his reason for splitting up the herd. He struggled with both thoughts until his brain could think no more and the pinpricks of light in the heavenly veil above disappeared into the blackness of sleep.

CHAPTER 7

The sense of a nearby presence awakened him. It was still dark. He lay motionless as he searched the surrounding darkness for any kind of movement against the backdrop of the stars, but the insistent night blinded him.

The blackness of the moonless sky made him smile with a new thought: the depth and breadth of his burgeoning hatred had been so severe that even the hombre who lived in the moon was afraid to show his face.

But something was near him. And quickly, all humor, however dark, left him the instant he realized that whatever lay out there hidden by the dark was coming closer.

He sniffed at the air. Nothing but the normal aromas of the desert filled his nostrils.

He sensed it, though. *What was moving up on him?*

His brain searched for the hidden answer. Most likely it would be a wolf. No. Not *a* wolf. Wolves in these parts traveled and hunted in packs. A coyote, then. They were often alone in their search for food. But he had been lying here all this time asleep. Why hadn't it already attacked him?

Just like Geronimo's splitting up of the herd, what was happening now made no sense. His right hand slowly inched toward the handle of his Colt in its holster lying near his head. With a flick of his thumb he released the leather hammer thong.

If it was a rattler, he was safe as long as he didn't move suddenly. Perhaps it was just looking to keep warm after a meal. Whatever it was, it was larger than an insect. He was sure of that. His senses heightened, his brain now keenly alert, he decided to jump up and confront the intruder. If it was a hungry pack of wolves or a coyote, they were going to be sorry.

Then an even more frightening thought came to him. What if it was Apache braves creeping up on him?

He decided that jumping up into the dark was not such a good idea after all. Instead, he would roll away from the noise, keeping low to the ground.

His hand tightened around the handle of his Colt, his thumb deftly finding the hammer, his index finger finding the trigger. He steadied himself and prepared to move.

Just then he heard a snort from the intruder. He snickered with relief. Tilly had inched closer to him; apparently the black desert night had made even her uncomfortable.

He stood up and reached out his hand toward the breathing sound. "You scared me, girl," he whispered, landing his hand on her nose. He rubbed it a few times and then set his forehead against hers while stroking her nose.

"It *is* dark out here, huh, girl? And as moonless nights go, I don't ever think I've seen it darker."

He dropped back down onto the sand and laid his back against the saddle.

"At first sunlight, Tilly, we'll follow them Apache ponies up into the Huachucas. That's what we'll do. We'll follow 'em and kill every last one of 'em. Ain't one we'll leave alive. Yes, sir. We'll kill 'em all kindsa dead, damn their eyes."

He was fully awake now. There would be no going back to sleep.

Once, long ago in another life, awaking early in the morning like this led to a cup of hot coffee and a newspaper, or a book, being read by the light of a crackling fire outside in the yard — his compassionate attempt to leave his family peacefully asleep as he delved into wonderful worlds created by the magical written words.

But that wasn't his life now. He looked toward the eastern horizon and saw the slightest hint of light. Sunrise was only a couple of hours away. It was still too dark to see anything. He had no fire, no book, no nothing except a burning resolve to get back to tracking the Apache horde.

Just then he heard a sound unlike any he had ever heard before. He could stand it no more. He rose up onto his knees and searched his saddlebag and found what he was looking for — a small candle. Right next to it was a box of strike-anywhere matches.

He pulled a match from the box, struck it to life, and lit the candle.

Surely, he thought, this small amount of light would not be seen from the hillside by any Apache lookout.

He held it up face high and then extended his arm out into the darkness. He could see nothing reflected in the light of the candle, not even the yellow eyes of a coyote. The light did not extend out far enough to be of much use to him, but it did give him some measure of confidence that all was well. At least relatively well.

Another odd sound, very faint, came from behind him. He turned quickly and found himself nearly nose to nose with the scowling face of an Apache brave. Before he could react, a blow to the back of his head ended any other thought.

———✦———

"My word!" said Gerald Thompson, closing the journal and resting it on his lap. "Mister Beckett was a conflicted and tormented soul. Was he not, sir?"

From his place at the campfire, Geronimo nodded.

"May I join you again?"

Geronimo nodded.

Thompson dropped next to him and wrung his hands against the heat of the fire.

"Amazing, sir. An amazin' story so far. So your braves captured him, huh?"

Geronimo nodded.

"I think it would have been over for me right there and then. I imagine he was pretty scared, too."

"Go read and find out," said Geronimo, still staring into the flames.

"I need a break. It is the most intense writin' I've ever read. It causes me heart palpitations and stifled breath. I swear, he is about as angry as I've ever known a man can be."

"His spirit burned hot then. I think the fire in him was too hot for anyone to cool."

"Again, sir, it must be an awful thing to live after seein' your family dead like that. How do you get through the remembrances now?"

"One moment after the next, Mister Thompson. Each step is taken with great effort. I think it will always be so for me. But then, I am not as strong as Connor Beckett."

"I beg to differ, sir. Twenty-two years held as a prisoner of war, and you still possess the graciousness to allow a newspaper reporter to share the warmth of a fire and fine conversation. You underestimate your worth and strength. And I believe that inspires even more greatness and strength, sir. I'm honored that you've allowed me to experience this."

Geronimo smiled.

"Kind words and an understanding smile, Mister Thompson. It is kind words and an understanding smile that get people like me through each day. Kind words ease the pains of memory. An understanding smile eases the loneliness."

"But you're not alone, sir."

"I am alone on this earth, Mister Thompson. I am all alone."

"But you have your new family with you here. How can you say that you are alone?"

"They are here, but they do not share the history of my life. They were not with me when I was in the desert running from the Blue-Coats. They did not see the hurt in my eyes for the suffering I had caused my people with my selfish desire for my freedom. They did not see the want of the old ways in my eyes. They did not feel the pressure of leadership weigh down upon their shoulders. I was alone then. I am alone now."

"I reckon I see how you might feel that way," said Thompson. "I've never been a leader, so I can't say that I understand the pressures of leadership. I live alone, but I can't say that I'm lonely. But you saved your people from extinction, Geronimo. They are here, alive, right now because of you. You are not alone, sir. You are most assuredly not alone. And what you did for your people took great courage and love. What you did demonstrates to me that you were not as selfish as you might think."

"Your eyes are open, Mister Thompson. Your ears are open. Your heart is open. And you are filled with kindness. It is a good thing. But you have never been filled with the crazy. You have never been alone with the crazy. It is the crazy that blocks all sight, all sound, all feeling, all kindness. After you have survived the crazy, you understand so much more."

"I don't know how to do that, Geronimo."

"Go read more, Mister Thompson. And you will learn about the crazy."

"I'll do that, sir."

Thompson immediately stood up and went back to the ramada chair and opened the journal again.

Even though filtered by the cloth over his face, the sunlight still burned Connor's eyes as he opened them. He tried to move, but his head felt as if it were about to explode. He ceased moving. He opened his mouth to speak, but all that sounded was a woeful groan. He realized that he had been gagged.

He relaxed and let his head fall back. It fell onto sand. His hands were tied behind him and his feet were bound tightly as well. His mind was a mass of jumbled thoughts, but any thoughts with hints of assembly told him he was in a very tight spot.

He heard the shuffling of sand around him and felt a firm hand drop onto the top of his head. Suddenly, sunlight flooded his eyes as a sack was yanked from his head.

As his squinting eyes slowly adjusted to the light, he found himself staring once again into the face of an enraged Apache brave. It might have been the same face as the night before, but he wasn't certain.

All he recalled from the night was big, white, fierce eyes staring back at him from out of the darkness. Connor blinked his eyes, hoping it was just a horrible but harmless specter.

It wasn't.

The terror of his reality became clear. He was a captive of the Apache — a prisoner of those he had been tracking with such vengeful purpose. Following that realization, he saw his life as instantly worthless, for he was about to experience all the horror and terror his family had had to endure before their own savage ends. His life was over. The only good thought that entered his brain was that soon he would be with his family again, in the next world. At least he hoped he would be allowed that privilege.

The brave, for all his fierceness, was a fine-looking specimen. He was young. Connor guessed him to be about twenty years old. His black hair was long and decorated with feathers, the sign of a worthy warrior. His face was simple, strong and smooth, a jaw set heavy and straight. His eyes were black as the night he had just awakened from. His teeth, bright white, were showing in a bitter sneer.

The brave's face was all that Connor could see. He heard a voice from somewhere behind the man. The Apache continued his stare in apparent defiance of the authoritative voice. Then his expression softened and he turned his face away.

Connor then saw the source of the voice. It belonged to none other than Geronimo himself. He recognized the face of the Apache chief from the photographs published in the newspapers. The crooked lines of his cruel-looking mouth, the weathered and cracked skin of his hardened face, the steely, piercing eyes expressing knowledge and wisdom, fear and terror — those knowing, resolute eyes that had seen things no White-Eye had ever seen, the photographs had captured it all perfectly.

Connor noted how the chief held his strong chin high, as if to boldly announce that it was right to fear this *wild man* of the Bedonkohe band of the Mescalero-Chiricahua Apaches, as the newspaper had so described him. The most dreaded man throughout this region, the man who had battled the Mexicans before, and the man who was now battling against the onslaught of the White-Eye infringing upon the sacred land of his ancestors, the man who would not surrender and become a prisoner. He was also the man who would determine both when and how Connor, the reviled would-be assassin now tied like the beast he was, would die, in what form and manner that terrible death would come. For it was widely known that Geronimo had a reputation for viciously torturing those he had captured and wanted dead.

Connor glared up at the fearsome chief defiantly. He might be dead before the hour was over, but like Geronimo, he would not surrender. He would have killed them all with his eyes alone if such a thing were possible.

Geronimo uttered a few words and the brave reached out and grabbed Connor by the shoulders and sat him up straight. As his hand brushed against Connor's shirt pocket, he noticed something stiff inside. The next thing Connor knew, the brave was pulling the picture of his family from the pocket.

Connor went ballistic, struggling against his bindings, his eyes squinted in anger, his voice, although still muffled by the gag, loudly cursing the most perverse profanity he could think of.

Unmoved by Connor's outburst, the brave stared at the photograph for a few seconds. Then Geronimo spoke and thrust out his hand. The brave grunted and placed the photograph into the weathered palm.

Geronimo brought the photograph closer. He studied it for several seconds and then his hard eyes returned to Connor's and pierced through him and straight into his soul. Still battling against his bindings, Connor stared back at the Apache chief defiantly, but then something shared in their mutual glowers caused him to stop struggling. He could not explain it to himself, but there was a sudden recognition, some kind of emotional connection with the chief on some hidden or indefinable ethereal level unfamiliar to him. Connor knew instantly that something unique had passed between them.

The old Indian turned his eyes back to the photograph for several more seconds, then he held it out to the brave and spoke again.

The brave took the photograph from the old man's hand and placed it back into Connor's shirt pocket carefully and gently.

Then Geronimo stepped forward and squatted down in front of Connor. He stared intently into his eyes again.

"The fire of hate burns strong in you," he said in English. "The fire has made you crazy. We cannot share good words while your heart is on fire and your ears are filled with the crazy."

Connor lunged at Geronimo and immediately found himself with the white burlap sack back over his head. After a few more choice but muffled curses, he felt a sharp pain against the side of his head and then all went black and silent again.

His head pounded as he opened his eyes and tried to focus them on his surroundings. He found himself hoping his head would explode off his shoulders just for the relief of ending his headache.

His eyes began to focus. The bag was still over his head so that all he could see was burlap. *Was he alone*? *Where was he*? *Where were his Apache captors*? No answers came to the silently asked questions.

He tried to move his hands, but they were still bound behind him. He tried to move his feet apart, but they also were still bound together.

He felt loose soil against his back, confirming that he was lying on the ground.

The heat was stifling. He had trouble breathing in the heat radiating off the sunbaked ground. His eyes burned from the heavy sweat pouring off his forehead and into his eyes.

He heard an indistinguishable noise behind him. As he turned his head toward the sound, a wave of nausea swept over him. Bile sped up his esophagus and he vomited. The mass struck the bag and splashed back onto his face. His head spun wildly. The pungent odor of his vomitus filled his senses. He swooned. The blackness returned.

He awakened, still lying on his back but now staring up into a star-filled sky. The night air was cool. He breathed easily. Someone had cleaned the vomitus off his face and chest, but the odor of it lingered.

His head still pounded, but his eyes were able to focus on the stars above him. All was quiet and still.

He turned his head to the side just as a hallucination materialized before him. His family was standing several yards away, beckoning to him. His vision blurred and the hallucination faded. A black mass stepped in front of him, blocking out the starlight. His eyes could not focus on the shape.

"You are still crazy," a voice said.

Connor tried to make sense of the words.

"Sleep, Crazy-Eyes. You are not yet worthy of words."

Connor tried to concentrate, but it was no use.

He tried to speak, but his words exited as only a mournful howl.

The darkness filled his mind once again.

When next he opened his eyes, he was still lying on the ground on his back, staring up into a now bright blue sky. His hands and feet were no longer bound.

He tightened his stomach muscles and sat up. His eyes came into focus. He recognized his surroundings. He was where he had been resting the night he was captured by the Apache. *But how many nights had passed since then? Where had he been? Had he been taken to their camp and now returned to his spot of capture?*

He twisted his head when he heard a noise behind him. It was Tilly. She had been hobbled.

It was as if his capture had been just a bad dream. He wanted to believe that it had been, but he had a raging headache still pressing against his temples.

Had he fallen and hit his head and, in an unconscious stupor, hallucinated his capture?

He searched the area immediately around him, but he saw nothing that could have caused him to black out had he fallen.

Try as he might, he could make no sense of his recent experience.

He stood up shakily and walked over to Tilly. A search of his saddlebags saw him supplied with food in the form of several tortilla-like shells wrapped around some kind of cooked meat. He checked his canteens. They were both filled to the brim, and two additional skins of fresh water were tied together and hung over his saddle's back housing.

He had not dreamed his capture. He had been a prisoner of Geronimo. *But why on earth had the Apache chief released him?*

Geronimo had freed him unharmed and even supplied him with food and water for his continuing journey. He must have ordered his braves to place him back where they had captured him. *But how many nights ago was that? One, two, perhaps more?* Time was a thing uncertain.

And where had they taken him? He recalled that the air was cooler there than where he stood now. So they must have transported him to their camp somewhere up in the surrounding hills of the Huachucas. They'd returned him to his point of capture, so they must be nearby. But he didn't really want to know how close they might be; he had been close enough already.

He checked all his firearms. They were loaded, and his extra ammo was untouched as well.

His eyes then fell to the sand. Apparently, while he was in the company of the Apache, the winds in the desert had been as still as the dead, for the tracks leading south and straight ahead remained quite visible. But he discovered that the tracks leading up into the Huachucas had been erased for quite a ways.

The Apache were allowing him to continue his murderous quest, but they had made it clear which direction they wanted him to go.

"Okay," he said aloud. "I understand."

CHAPTER 8

Connor mounted Tilly and reined her in the direction of the tracks that remained intact, not knowing where or to whom they might lead.

He had lied to himself when he'd claimed to understand. He didn't understand any of this.

The thought of Geronimo allowing him to live at all was strange enough, but for the chief to order his braves to place him back on the trail unharmed and fully supplied seemed completely unreal.

It would take a while to reason out the answer to this conundrum, but he was certainly glad for the opportunity to do so. He had heard so many stories about those who had been captured by Geronimo — by those who foolishly believed that they had escaped the control of the Apache chief.

No one ever escaped Geronimo. They were either tortured and killed or they were allowed to leave. It was only self-deluded fools who held the belief that they had been clever enough to escape the clutches of that murderous animal. If one had gained his release, one could be sure that it was the unexplained will of Geronimo that had allowed him the freedom.

Connor noted that the tracks were all from shod horses, including the horses of the riders, and that could only mean that white men were with his herd.

He immediately reasoned it out. Geronimo was telling him that he was looking for white devils.

The tracks continued southeast and stayed straight and true for the whole day, until late that afternoon he came across yet another divergence.

He climbed down and squatted over them, studying them closely. Three horses had split off from the main body of the herd. From the depths of the prints in the sand it appeared that they were mounted by heavy men.

The reason for them to split off, especially out in this part of the desert, was again lost on him. But then, being bewildered was becoming a normal way of life for him now.

Once more, indecision filled his head. But unlike before, he quickly settled on following the divergent tracks.

He remounted Tilly and reined her in their direction.

Two hours had passed when he came upon a cold campfire.

Sliding down from his saddle, he squatted next to the cinders and placed his hand just over them, searching for any remnant of heat. There was none. He figured the fire had been out for at least a day, with sand having been kicked over the cinders, partially covering them.

Then something caught his eye next to the fire pit. Assorted insects were swarming a particular spot on the ground. He swept them away and noticed the patch of dried blood.

Someone had lain there and bled, forming a pool which had, for the most part, percolated down into the sand.

Someone had been wounded.

He moved more sand and discovered the tip of a dark blue bandana, soaked with blood.

He pulled it out and looked at it. It was clear to him that it belonged to a white man. Indians didn't use bandanas.

There was now no doubt about what the Apaches were trying to make him understand. Then he recalled the two dead horses he had run across on his way home from Tombstone.

White men had gone to his cabin, tortured and killed his family, and taken his horses. Now he knew he was on the true trail of those he needed to unleash his revenge against.

More made sense now. There must have been a gun battle and one of them was wounded. Maybe they had battled the Apache. *But why the divergent trail? And what about that torn bit of leather with the Apache markings on it that he'd found in his cabin?*

Perhaps the Apaches were trying to deflect responsibility onto white men. They were a tricky and sneaky people. *But why would they do that?* It certainly couldn't be because they feared his wrath. They could have killed him at any moment while they held him captive. Nothing along that line of reasoning his mind came up with made any sense.

So where was he being led now, he wondered. Then he recalled the small settlement everyone called Buenavista. It wasn't much, really; a trading post and a few ramshackle houses. He recalled riding through it some years back. Perhaps that was where the tracks would lead him. They were certainly heading in the right direction.

He heeled Tilly's belly to find what answers he could.

Whoever he was tracking had at least a two-day lead on him, maybe more, depending on how long he had been unconscious while in the hands of the Apache.

They weren't moving very fast. Of course, nothing moved quickly out here in this desert anyway, but perhaps they were slowed down even more because of the one who was wounded. Or perhaps the reason was that they had no extra horses, now that they had been separated from the herd. With the lack of water, they would have to keep the pace slow or risk killing their horses and be stranded out in the desert — a desert far more wicked than they could ever hope to be.

But three men had surely separated from the main body. *How many more had gone on with the herd? How many more would he have to kill after he had finished with these three men?* More unanswerable questions filled his brain.

Connor wondered how those men initially saw the herd of horses they had stolen from him. *Did they steal them as a marketable commodity? Were they just a bunch of horse thieves who took advantage of an easy opportunity? Or, considering the direction they were heading, did they steal them simply as replacements for their horses? But why would they need replacements? Perhaps they were rushing away, attempting to flee justice for other crimes? Maybe that's how the one became wounded?* Fighting against a posse will do that sometimes.

Connor supposed that a justifiable reason for rushing through a hostile desert would be to avoid a hangman's noose for the crimes of murder and horse theft. And rushing across this desert, under these conditions, tends to kill horses.

But dash as they may, he vowed to stay the course until he found every last one of them and put them in their graves.

They were gambling, though, for the desert provided no grazing for the horses. They were already hungry if not starving by now. They had to be already weakened by hunger and thirst. They couldn't be pushed much harder or they would be of little use when the horse thieves needed them. If the men weren't careful, they would end up with only a herd of dead horses as their replacements. And a dead horse wouldn't get anyone too far.

The afternoon sun was already blisteringly hot. Connor could tell that it was only going to get hotter. The extra skins of water given to him by the Apache, at Geronimo's behest, would become more than a little important as the day wore on.

Tilly, well rested, was feeling spirited. Connor surmised that she wanted to catch up to those demons as badly as he did. Perhaps she harbored her own concept of justice. Perhaps it was all only in Connor's mind, but the results were the same: Tilly wanted to run, but Connor couldn't allow her to do that.

Connor had hunted men before, although it had been many years ago, during his more exuberantly youthful days during the war. He'd had a lot more vigor and tenacity back then. He could ride longer in the saddle. He could handle the abuse to his body better. He'd adapted better during those distant times to extreme changes in weather. But those days were well behind him. Only the driving force of his hatred kept him glued to his saddle now.

His mind had drifted off and he nearly ambled past the signs in the sand.

Bringing Tilly to an abrupt stop, he slid down off the saddle and walked to the disturbance in the sand. The tracks were very different now. The horses were dragging their hooves. They were tired. They were thirsty. They were in bad shape. It wouldn't be long before he'd find the bodies of dead horses.

They continued more east than southeast, like the main body, but still in the general direction of Buenavista. He crouched down onto his haunches as his eyes scanned the tracks outward until they were interrupted by a sharp, steep rise about a half mile ahead.

"I'm comin' for ya, fellas. For nothin' more than hate's sake, I'm comin' for ya."

Connor studied the tracks some more.

"You ain't far ahead, are ya? Your tracks are fresher. Your horses are about to drop out from under ya, aren't they? That's just fine, fellas. Stay with your dead horses. I'll be with you shortly to finish *you* off."

Connor arose and remounted Tilly, reining her toward the rise.

He rode in silence until he neared the summit of the rise, then he reined Tilly to stop and dismounted, pulling his Winchester from its scabbard.

As he neared the summit, he went to his belly as before. He removed his hat and finished inching up to the summit until, peering over it, he saw what he had hoped to see.

Three riders in the distance, about a quarter mile ahead, their horses walking very slowly across the blistering sand as they sweltered in the heat of midday.

Connor noted one of them teetering in his saddle. He assumed it was the wounded one, but it could just as easily have been any of them feeling the effects of sun sickness.

"Sick or wounded, fella, your pain ain't nothin' to me. Just means you're in no kinda condition to put up much of a fight. That's just fine."

One of the horses stumbled. It shifted sharply to the left and then to the right. The rider tried to right himself, but the horse shifted sharply again, then fell over onto the ground. It was done for.

Through field glasses retrieved from his saddlebag, Connor watched with delight as the fallen man picked himself up from the ground. He dusted himself off, pulled his rifle from its scabbard, cocked it, and fired a single shot into his horse's head.

"Too bad, fella. But you'll soon follow your mount."

Connor thought for a moment. Perhaps he might aid in the other two horses' demise with a nudge or two.

He aimed his rifle at the dead horse, knowing it was out of effective range for the bullet but not the report of the rifle.

He knew that the three wilting men would hear the rifle shot and try to heel their horses into a galloping escape. The horses were spent, though. Connor could see that clearly. They'd had no water for a long time.

They would try to run, but they were dehydrated and their energy was spent. They wouldn't make it very far before they would tumble to the ground as the last horse had.

The men would have to either turn and fight or try to run themselves. Torturing them drifted back into his mind once again. If he wanted, he could make those three men suffer terribly before he mercifully put a bullet into each of their hearts.

But for Connor, mercy was a long way off. Kindness was altogether absent, and compassion found no way into his heart or mind. He just wanted them to live long enough to know who it was ending their wicked existence. Torture took a long time and a lot of patience to do it right. But what he needed was information — information about where the others were heading. He didn't expect these three to give up too much too fast, but he would create an environment in which they would want to do it freely. To accomplish that, of course, meant that he would have to resort to various methods of inducement. Yes, that would be his only means of extracting the information he'd need to find the others.

Once he'd obtained the necessary information, he could abandon his arduous tracking effort and ride straight to the rest of the men. Then he would bring a terrible wrath down upon them and finish his earthly purpose.

Connor squeezed the trigger. The rifle exploded. The bullet struck the ground close enough to put the men into a panic.

The horseless rider jumped up behind one of his partners and the two horses leapt into a gallop under the heeled urgings of their masters.

Connor smiled. It had gone perfectly.

Within minutes the two horses climbed another distant rise and disappeared over it.

Connor slowly stood up, dusted the sand from himself, and moved toward Tilly without any sense of haste.

The way those horses had bolted away, he knew he'd find them shortly, sprawled out on the sand, and three men trying desperately to run across the desert.

He drank a large swallow of water from his canteen and then, using his hat as a bowl, watered Tilly. They were in no rush. They had plenty of time.

After a moment, Connor remounted Tilly and the two of them leapt into an easy trot toward the fleeing strangers and the first downed horse.

CHAPTER 9

Connor's search of the first horse gave him nothing new except empty saddlebags and an empty rifle scabbard.

He remounted Tilly.

Minutes later, they reached the summit of the second rise in a very easy gait.

From atop Tilly, Connor saw that his clever ploy had been rewarded handsomely.

Out in the desert, about two or three hundred yards ahead, he saw the bodies of the two horses, separated from each other by some two hundred feet.

Ahead of the horses, perhaps two hundred yards more, staggered three men along the sandy landscape. One of the men hobbled along and supported himself with his rifle. Connor surmised that he was the wounded one.

The other two must have abandoned their belongings, for they carried nothing in their hands, not even their canteens. Connor reasoned that they weren't too far behind their horses in terms of giving up the ghost.

He arrived at the second downed horse.

He dropped from Tilly's saddle and inspected the saddlebags. He found tied bundles of bills, perhaps one inch thick, in varying denominations, from one dollar to ten dollars.

There were five bundles in all. He picked them up and surveyed them a moment or two and then let them slip from his hand to the sand.

He had no use for the money. Money only aided the living.

His continued search yielded nothing useful. A cartridge box was broken and empty. The canteen slipped over the saddle horn was empty. A well-used Winchester rifle was still in its scabbard. He pulled it free and checked it. It was empty, which confirmed why it was left behind. Carrying it would only mean extra weight for the man whose own weight was already too heavy for the heat. Connor dropped the rifle to the sand.

He grabbed Tilly's reins and tugged her forward to the third horse. He discovered much of the same, but in one of the saddlebags he found something else. It was a small square of quilted cloth. It looked familiar to him, but he couldn't quite place it.

He studied it. There was a memory of it set somewhere in the back of his mind, but he found it impossible to yank it to the front of his brain.

It was the wrong material for a bandana and it was much too small anyway. He was about to stuff it into his shirt pocket when the memory of it smacked him hard.

"Rebecca!" he shouted. "Rebecca's blanket!"

The square of material was the blanket for his daughter's doll, Rebecca.

Rage surged through him like a lightning bolt. He reeled.

The blanket confirmed his worst thoughts. These men had been to his cabin. Whether or not they had anything to do with his family's murder, he couldn't say, but they had been there. They at least had seen his family.

A bullet ripped into the sand several yards from him. He looked up and saw one of the men shouldering a rifle several hundred yards away. He saw the muzzle flash, and a second later another bullet landed woefully short.

Connor didn't wait for a third shot.

He reached up to his own rifle and yanked it from its scabbard. Then he laid himself out on the sand, adjusted the sight carefully, aimed steadily, and squeezed the trigger.

The rifle exploded loudly. A second later, the man with the rifle dropped and didn't move. The other two men dashed away from the skilled sniper.

Connor cocked the rifle and aimed at them, but he didn't fire, remembering that he needed information from them before sending them to the next world. He let them run, knowing that they wouldn't get far in their condition.

He grabbed Tilly's reins and guided her out to the fallen man.

When he reached him, he saw two bullet holes, one in the side of his belly, wrapped but still oozing. The other, through the left shoulder, was fresh and bleeding profusely. That one was the result of Connor's shot.

The man lay still, but his eyelids fluttered involuntarily. He was alive — barely.

Connor kicked the rifle away from his hands and squatted next to him. He pulled the square of quilted cloth from his pocket and held it up so the man could see it, but he said nothing.

The man regained control of his eyelids and looked at the bit of dangling cloth. His eyes opened wide in recognition.

"It wasn't me. I had nothin' to do with it."

"But you know who did it, don't ya."

The man shook his head no.

Connor reached out with the muzzle of his rifle and pressed it against the man's wounded shoulder.

He yelped.

"Where's the doll?"

"I don't know. I don't know!"

Connor punched the muzzle into the shoulder wound again.

"One more time, you sumbitch. Where's the doll?"

"I don't know."

"Liar! Who did it? Who killed my family?"

"Cutter. He ordered it. It was Cutter. He's got the doll, too."

"Who's Cut…"

In a flash, it all became clear to him. He recalled reading in the *Record-Epitaph* about the

Thaddaeus "Cutter" Brown Gang that had robbed the bank in Tucson and were escaping south.

The Brown Gang explained the bundle of money, the stolen horses, his family. It explained everything.

"Cutter Brown?"

The man nodded.

Connor pushed the muzzle of his rifle up under the man's chin and squeezed the trigger, liberating the man's brains from his skull.

He then glared up at the men still dashing away from him. He saw them stop and turn their heads back toward him. They had heard the shot.

Then they resumed running.

He mounted Tilly and heeled her forward toward the fleeing men.

He allowed Tilly to walk easy. But it was not for the sake of being gentle or reassuring that he did so. On the contrary, there was a cold, methodical, calculated reason for the slow pace.

He was instilling the ultimate fear into the men running away as he steadily followed them.

Several times they stopped, looked back at him, and then dashed away. He dogged them relentlessly.

One of the men finally stopped, turned, and raised his revolver. Connor saw the flash. The bullet dropped into the sand tens of yards in front of him. He ignored the threat and continued toward the man.

The outlaw raised his gun again and fired. Once more the bullet fell short. Then he saw the man aim again, but there was no flash. The man tossed the revolver to the ground. Connor smiled. The fool had spent his last two rounds in a wasted effort.

They stood still as statues staring at Connor until he was finally within earshot of them. Connor stopped Tilly and stared at them.

"Who the hell *are* you, mister?" asked the man who had tossed his revolver.

Connor ignored the man's question and continued staring at them.

The man then jolted and backed up quickly.

"The rider!" he shouted. "He's on a pale horse!"

"It's a palomino," said the other man.

"It's pale enough for me," the first man said, still moving backward.

"What the devil you talkin' 'bout?"

"Oh, Lordy. It's Death!"

"What?"

"Ain't yer mama ever read to ya from the Good Book?"

"My mama was a whore in a saloon."

"'*And I looked, and behold a pale horse: and his name that sat on him was Death, and Hell followed with him.*'"

"I ain't never heard that. Yer makin' that up."

"It's Death, I tell ya. And he's comin' for *us*!"

"Well, maybe you. Not me. I ain't done nothin' to deserve this."

"Yer stupid, Charlie. And yer a damn liar."

"Yeah, well, maybe so, Gabe, but I ain't no coward."

Charlie lifted his rifle at the still specter, aimed, and fired. He missed cleanly, the bullet whizzing past Connor to his left. He showed no fear of Charlie's bullet and continued staring at the men.

In the thick air, it was as if he was standing right in front of them, hearing every word of their shouted conversation.

"He's a steady one. I'll give 'im that."

"It's *Death*, Charlie!"

Gabe turned and dashed away.

"It's a damn palomino, you moron."

He cocked his rifle, aimed, and fired again. The bullet went wide right this time.

"Come on, stranger," shouted Charlie at Connor.

Charlie cocked the rifle, aimed, and squeezed the trigger. The hammer fell harmlessly against metal. The click surprised him.

"Damn it all!" He threw the rifle down, tugged his revolver from its holster, aimed, and fired. The bullet slammed harmlessly into the sand far short of its intended target.

He cocked, aimed, and pulled the trigger. Click. The revolver was out of ammunition as well.

That revolver then went the way of the other two guns — into the sand. Charlie turned and ran away, trying to catch up to the man he called Gabe.

Connor smiled grimly.

An hour passed without Connor doing anything more than simply following the men, keeping them within earshot, but no closer.

Charlie finally stumbled to the sand. He rose up onto his knees and looked back at Connor.

Connor reined Tilly to a stop and just stared at the exhausted man kneeling in the sand. He maintained his distance, some fifty yards away — taunting him — frightening him.

Charlie stood up and screamed at Connor.

"Who the hell *are* you?"

Connor did not reply.

"What do you want?" screamed the man.

Connor only stared coldly at him.

The man started walking toward Connor. But Connor reined Tilly backward, maintaining his distance.

The man saw Tilly backing up. Realizing that he would not get any closer, he screamed again.

"*Who are you?*"

Connor stopped Tilly and stared.

"Why are you doing this?"

Connor did not respond verbally. Instead, he pulled his rifle from its scabbard and sat the butt end against his thigh, the muzzle sticking up in the air.

The man saw it and stumbled backward until he fell to the ground.

"Maybe you *are* Death, like Gabe says," shouted Charlie, "but you're a coward son of a bitch, too."

Connor ignored Charlie's taunt, but then remembered something very important — a spring of fresh water about a three-hour walk ahead.

Another torture filled his thoughts.

"Three hours," Connor said in a low whisper. "Can I push 'em another three hours? Can I haunt 'em that much longer?"

He glanced up into the late afternoon sky.

"About nightfall, Sarah, honey," he murmured. "That's about when we should get to the spring. I'd like to give them a touch of hope before I take it all from them."

He pulled a bandana from his pocket and wiped his face dry.

"They'll think they've been given a reprieve with fresh water, Sarah. I'll let 'em think they'll make it outa this desert alive. And then I'll pounce on 'em and take joy in sendin' 'em to Hell one piece at a time. I'll make 'em dead there, honey. I promise you they'll die screamin'."

Approximately three hours later, just as Connor had predicted, he saw Charlie drop to his knees at the spring and plunge his face into the cool water.

He reveled in the coolness of the spring as if he had no thought in his head of the haunting specter relentlessly trailing him.

Gabe soon did the same.

Then Connor heard them laugh. It was the first laughter he had heard from them. He smiled. He wanted them to laugh. He wanted them to feel hope.

They refreshed themselves as Connor stared at them from behind a large boulder.

They did not look well by any stretch of the imagination. In fact, they looked very sick. And they were sick — badly sun sick. But for the briefest of moments, he let them think they would be all right.

And that's exactly what they thought.

"We gonna be just fine, Gabe."

"Yes we is, Charlie. I thought I might turn to dust back there a while ago."

Gabe thrust his head upward. He turned it from side to side as if searching for something.

"Where'd he go?" he asked.

"Who?"

"That demon followin' us."

Charlie looked up.

"I was so close to givin' up the ghost the last hour or so, I plumb forgot about 'im."

"I don't see 'im. Do you?" asked Gabe.

Charlie's head jerked around as his eyes searched for Connor.

"No, Gabe. No, I don't. You think he was some kinda mirage?"

"He was there behind us all the time, Charlie. You saw 'im. Don't tell me you didn't."

"I saw 'im. At least I thought I saw 'im."

"I saw 'im, too. But I don't see 'im now."

"Maybe he *was* just in our heads, Gabe. Maybe the sun done cooked our brains and we was just seein' what we was afraid to see."

"But what about Jeb? What about that shooter that took Jeb down?"

"Maybe it was a posse. Maybe they gave up the chase. I don't know anymore, Gabe."

"Then who was we seein' behind us?"

"Maybe nothin'. Maybe the sun was playin' tricks on us, bein' poorly like we was. Maybe we was hit with the sun sickness."

"Maybe… I guess so. But we's okay now, ain't we, Charlie?"

"We sure is. We gonna be just fine."

"That depends on your definition of *fine*, fellas," said Connor, stepping out into the open from behind a boulder, rifle muzzle pointed directly at the outlaws.

Charlie took three steps backward. Connor fired a round near his feet and re-cocked the rifle.

"Don't be stupid," said Connor. "Don't be stupider than you already have been, that is. You can't outrun a bullet."

Charlie stopped and raised his hands up near his shoulders.

"Don't shoot! Don't shoot! I surrender, Marshal."

"I ain't a marshal."

"You're not? What kinda lawman are you, then?"

"Well, Charlie, I ain't the law at all."

"What you want with us, then? How do ya know our names?"

Connor pulled the square of cloth from his shirt pocket and held it up for them to see.

"Overheard you boys talkin' a bit ago, callin' each other by name, and I'm here about this, fellas."

"That was Jeb's, mister."

"I didn't find it in Jeb's saddlebag, Charlie. If that's who it was I shot earlier. No, sir. I found it in one of your saddlebags. The question is, which one of you is it? That's what I'm gonna find out real soon."

"What about Jeb, mister? We heard a shot. Is Jeb okay?"

"He's fine, Gabe. Lost his head over the matter some. But he's just fine now, I reckon."

"Oh Jesus, Charlie. He *is* Death! He's gonna kill us, too."

"Listen, mister. We had nothin' to do with that mess," said Charlie.

"What mess is that?"

"That mess back yonder. The reason you's here now. *That* mess."

"What are you talkin' about, Charlie."

"That mess back at the ranch. That's what I'm talkin' about. It wasn't us. We didn't have nothin' to do with it."

"Nothin' to do with it, huh? Then what were you doin' with Miss Rebecca's blanket?"

"Miss who?"

"This square of cloth, Charlie. This was Miss Rebecca's blanket. Miss Rebecca is a doll. Belonged to my daughter, Emma. If you had nothin' to do with it, what are you doin' with her blanket?"

"Ah, geez, mister. It was on the ground. I picked it up. I thought it was a handkerchief or somethin'."

"A handkerchief. Does it look like a handkerchief to you?"

"It was pretty, mister. I...I...just... It was pretty. I didn't do nothin' to your family. Me and Gabe was outside with the ponies."

"There's money, mister," said Gabe. "There's a whole lot of money back in them saddlebags. It's yours. All of it. Just let us go. We won't say nothin' about it. We got it from a bank in Tucson we robbed. They...they won't miss it none."

"I found it," said Connor.

"You did?"

"I sure did, Gabe. In a saddlebag. Big as day. All them bills just starin' back at me."

"Well...," Charlie chuckled nervously. "Well, there it is, then. You keep it. We don't want it."

You're just a chuckle bag, ain't ya, Charlie? You findin' all of this funny, are ya?"

"No, sir. Ain't nothin' funny 'bout any of this."

"Then why are you laughin'? You think I'm funny?"

"No, sir. You ain't funny."

"You think I'm some kinda jokester?"

"I said no, sir. You surely ain't no kinda jokester."

"Then I ask you again, Charlie. Why ya laughin'?"

"It's just my nerves. I do that sometimes. Laugh, I mean. When I git real nervous, I chuckle a bit. It's a condition."

"A condition. You got a nervous condition?"

"Yes, sir. Right now I sure do."

"What are you nervous about?"

"About what you're gonna do to me."

"What do you think I'm gonna do to you, Charlie?"

"I think you're gonna kill me."

"Now, why would I do that?"

"'Cause your family was kilt by the boys and you come lookin' for revenge."

"I reckon you're spot on there, Charlie."

"Go back and get the money, mister. You can have it all. It's like…like…you know what they calls it when someone been done wrong."

"You mean compensation, Charlie?"

"Yes, sir. That's it. Compensation. We don't want none of it."

"Me either, fellas. It'll probably just rot out there where I left it."

"You left it?" asked Charlie.

"What did you do that for?" asked Gabe. "Are you crazy?"

"Maybe, Gabe. A little, I guess. But, fellas, I told ya already. I ain't here about the money. We ain't gonna need money where we're gonna end up, boys. Ain't nothin' you can buy in Hell."

"Listen, mister," said Charlie, "we didn't wanna be a part of killin' yer family. It was Cutter gone mad that did it. It was him that decided on such doins'. We was just outside watchin' the horses."

"He raped my wife and daughter alone? He killed my family all by himself, did he?"

"Well, no, sir. Not by hisself. He did your wife for sure. But Jeb helped some, I guess. That's what he went on and bragged about, anyway. But you done kilt him already."

"Yeah," said Gabe. "And Tugger, he did your daughter. Him…him and McCarthy. They ain't no good, them two. I ain't never liked neither of 'em none myself. They only came on recent with us. I didn't know 'em too good."

"But you did nothin' to stop 'em, Gabe. You didn't lift a finger to help my family, did ya?"

"We couldn't, mister," said Charlie. "Cutter was mad with the frenzy. He'd a kilt us just the same if we woulda tried. We're glad to be away from 'im, to be honest with ya. We're goin' straight from here on out. I swear."

"I believe you, Charlie. I do," said Connor.

"That's good, mister. 'Cause I don't want no kinda bad blood between us. It was a real shame what happened to your family. I don't condone such things happenin' to good folks."

"Then why didn't you stop Cutter? Why didn't you kill 'im for the reward money?"

"Cutter's real mean, mister. What if I missed? He'd skin me alive."

"So, you're a coward and you let him torture and kill my whole family. Is that what you're sayin'?

"It's true, mister. I'm coward as they come. And it's the straight and narrow for me from now on. Yes, sir. Goin' straight as an arrow, I swear it."

"Me, too," said Gabe. "What he said. I'm a coward, too. And I'm goin' straight."

"I do believe you, fellas. I believe you're goin' straight. Straight to Hell. But first, we're gonna have us some fun."

CHAPTER 10

Connor sat stirring a twig in the embers of the campfire.

Across from him sat Gabe and Charlie, tied firmly hand and foot, quiet as field mice. Their hollow eyes were fixed on Connor Beckett, for he had not uttered a word for over an hour.

He neither threatened them nor gave them solace. There was only ominous silence from him.

They had given up asking the big man any questions a while ago. He had ignored each one, as if he didn't hear one word they said.

Connor finally stirred and expelled a single long breath. With his eyes fixed on the glowing coals, he spoke:

"It was on a trail somewhere up near the headwaters of the Brazos, many years ago, that I came upon him. A real hard man — about the hardest man I ever met. I was much younger then... Your bindin's ain't too tight, are they, fellas?"

Gabe and Charlie sat still as rocks. Even if the bindings were too tight, they weren't going to take the chance of upsetting the maniac sitting across from them. Their eyes open wide in terror, the two men remained silent, staring at Connor Beckett, wondering where the story was heading — hoping the big man would continue talking. The longer he talked, the longer they would live.

"I'll take your silence as a 'no.' Anyway, he had a man hog-tied and lyin' next to him when I came upon 'im. Not much different than you are now, come to think on it. He was good enough to me, though. Invited me to sit nearby and share his fire and even offered me a nice hot cup of freshly brewed coffee while he shared some of his story with me.

"The tied-up man had done somethin' awful to the hard man's wife. That's what he said, anyway. He didn't get specific, and I had the good manners not to pry, you understand. But whatever it was he did, it stirred the hard man to a real ugly and violent manner. That much was plain enough to see.

"He added a lot of wood to the fire until he got it real high and hot. He cooked me up some more of that fine coffee. It was good, too. Then he fed that man into the flames feet first, a few inches at a time. Took the man some time to die. Most of the night, in fact. He screamed a lot. Loud, too. But even after he died, it didn't stop the hard man from continuin' to feed his body into the fire. Took the rest of the night and a good part of the mornin' to burn him down to ashes. Say, would you fellas care for some coffee?"

Although seemingly the stronger of the two, it was Charlie who first rolled his eyes and passed out.

Gabe remained alert and silent, surreptitiously twisting against the ropes. His eyes never left Connor Beckett's face, even though Connor could see that the man was edging toward blind panic. He could make out plain and simple the fear going wild behind those wide-open eyes.

Connor nodded and chuckled. "I'll take that as no to the coffee, Gabe."

He studied the unconscious man.

"Looks like ol' Charlie took my story a bit hard."

Connor shifted his position and poked his twig deeper into the embers.

"I'll tell ya, it was a tough thing to watch it happenin'. I can still hear them awful bloodcurdlin' screams sometimes when it gets real quiet... You sure them bindin's ain't too tight for ya?

"Anyway, I remember the look on that hard man's face in the midst of all that bellowin'. It was like he was hearin' a sweet song playin' in his ears, just for him. I learned a lot about the nature of both fear and anger that night, Gabe."

Connor fell quiet as he stirred the coals for several seconds. Then he looked directly into Gabe's face. "You ever smelt a man burn in a fire? It's a horrible smell, I'll tell you that. Once you smell human flesh burn, you don't never forget it. But can you imagine smellin' your *own* flesh as it cooks and sizzles. That's got to be downright unnervin'. Wouldn't you agree, Gabe?"

Connor Beckett fell silent again. His eyes dropped back to the embers he continued to stir.

After a time, he looked back up at Gabe. The outlaw kept his eyes glued to Connor Beckett's as sweat streamed down off his face in several small rivulets.

Connor returned his eyes to the embers and sat quiet and still for some time, staring hypnotically at the remains of the fire. Finally, he sighed mournfully.

Gabe maintained his terrified stare, although now there was a discernible and growing sense of urgency on his face.

"Right now," Connor whispered, "I'm thinkin' we need more wood for this fire. What do you think, Gabe?"

"Ah, Jesus, mister. Please don't do that. I regret my part in that business. I really do. I'm a good man, I really am. I got forced into that bit of nastiness. Cutter said he'd kill me if I didn't take part in it. Truly, mister, I didn't mean no harm. I've been filled with deep remorse about it ever since it happened."

"I'm sure you have," replied Connor. "I believe you. I truly do. I bet you're regrettin' *everythin'* right now. In fact, at this very moment I bet you're regrettin' even havin' been born. No doubt about it. We all live with regret, Gabe. Some more'n others, I expect. Life, it seems, is just plum full of regrets, but that don't stop bad things from happenin' to us, does it?"

Connor rose to his feet and began gathering up more wood. "Yes, sir. Life is full of regrets... Well, I reckon it's time to get this fire growed up some. Your feet toasty enough, are they?"

Gabe's eyes rolled up and then *he* passed out.

Nearly thirty minutes later Gabe's eyes inched open. Earlier, Charlie had returned to the land of the conscious to find Connor stoking the fire with fresh twigs. Connor cut him a wicked grin and Charlie passed out again.

As Gabe slowly regained full consciousness, his eyes began darting about in search of something recognizable, and then, seizing upon Connor Beckett, opened wide in astonishment. He bolted upright and stared down at his legs. They were exactly where they should be, below his waist. He saw his boots, also exactly where they should be — still on his feet.

The fire was sizzling and crackling and he had not yet been fed into it.

"You...you ain't burned me up."

"I reckon not, since you ain't burnt yet," answered Connor matter-of-factly.

"You said you was. You started gatherin' up wood."

"I said no such thing. I said we needed to grow up the fire. It wouldn't be good to have the fire go out on us out here. If we let the fire go out, we'd be chilled to the bone instead of nice and toasty like we are. Besides that, without a fire, we'd have all manner of hungry critters upon us in no time."

"You ain't gonna burn me, then?"

"I ain't come to no conclusion just yet on what I'm gonna do with you two." A sly grin crept across his face. "Would you like to burn?"

"NO!" came the instant response.

"Then tell me where I can find the rest of your gang. Heck, I might even let you live through this if you do."

"I can't tell ya. They'd kill me for sure."

"RATTLESNAKE EYES!" shouted Connor.

"Rattle... What? What you talkin' about?"

"Rattlesnake eyes," repeated Connor. "You ever seen 'em up close?"

"No, sir. Can't say I have."

"They're pure black. They look dead — no emotion. It's like they'd just as soon see ya dead as alive. Ya can't reason with rattlesnake eyes."

Connor stretched out his left foot and kicked at a burlap sack. As his toe tapped it, the distinctive rattle vibrated loudly.

"My friend here stopped by a while ago, I guess for the water."

"Ah, no," pleaded Gabe. "Please don't. Please. I beg you."

"I reckon my wife and kids did some beggin', too, huh? But it didn't help 'em none, did it? You tell me where I can find the rest of your bunch, or you'll get an up-close meetin' with ol' snake eyes here. Or..."

Connor looked at him and smiled. "I guess I could burn on ya some first."

"You ain't got no heart, mister."

"Did have. Once. A while ago. Seein' my family dead like they was, though, sorta killed it. I believe I buried a piece of it in each one of their graves."

CHAPTER 11

The chill of the night had fallen across the desert, but it wasn't all that cold.

Still, Charlie sat nearly frozen by the warming campfire with the numbing paralysis of fear. He was seated against a boulder, his feet and hands bound securely to the sharpened stake driven deep into the sand in front of him. The bindings, wet leather thongs, would tighten as the leather dried, preventing him from doing anything but sit and shiver with fright.

Lying next to him was Gabe. Gabe was dead. Rattlesnake venom will do that to you, especially after so many bites about the head, face, and neck by an angry and frightened desert viper.

That was the price of his silence. Or his ignorance.

Connor had been patient with Gabe. He'd asked him to reveal the whereabouts of Cutter Brown. Gabe said he didn't know where Cutter was just then. Connor had asked him where the leader of the gang had planned to go and hide out until the reaction to the bank robbery up in Tucson had died down. Gabe couldn't say for sure what Cutter Brown had in mind for their escape. Connor was not pleased with Gabe's answers.

Still, Connor was patient. As patient as a man driven to murderous revenge can be, that is. But even a patient man reaches the end of his patience when he needs information. Absent any useful answers from a murderous, lying outlaw, Connor could see no further use for him. And a sack containing a riled-up rattlesnake, placed over a head and tied off, can produce only one end.

That is the circumstance into which Charlie had regained consciousness. Witnessing such an event tends to sharpen the mind and loosen the tongue.

Charlie admitted that he and Gabe had taken full part in the rape and murder of Connor's family. He also recalled Cutter saying that there was a canyon just south of Buenavista that provided good protection from a posse and the like. He figured to wait out all the hullabaloo over the bank robbery and then drift on to the nice life all that money would allow. At least until he needed more money.

Connor departed the campsite, promising to return and cut him free. But that was two hours ago, at least.

Still, he expected Connor to return as he had said he would. From his dealings with the crazed man so far, he had, for well or ill, kept his word.

He didn't for a moment expect to live through the night, but he did expect to be freed from the bindings before something inhuman came into the camp.

By the end of the third hour, he wondered if Connor had lied to him after all.

No. He figured Connor was only teaching him a lesson — a departing lesson to be taken into the next world. For now, though, he had to wait. He had to be patient.

But wait as he could only do, minutes still slipped by and by. And Connor had yet to return.

By that time, the fire had largely burned itself out. Only dim embers remained to give any kind of light and warmth.

The chilling, isolating blackness of the night was something he had never really thought about before that evening. Filling quickly with all of his regrets, it had become a blacker night than he had ever seen before, but at that moment, no blacker than his hopes.

He heard a noise off to his left — a slight shifting of sand. There was weight to it.

"Okay," he cried out. "I know yer out there. I can hear ya. I learnt my lesson. Cut me free and just kill me. I can't take this no more, mister. Yeah, I admit it again. I had a hand in killing yer family. I had yer wife, too. So did Gabe. I admit it all. I'm ready to meet my maker. Just cut me loose and don't let the night varmints at me. I beg you, mister."

There was no response from who he was certain was Connor Beckett come back to finish him off.

"Have mercy, mister. I'm beggin' ya. This ain't right."

Still no response. The sound drew closer until it was only a few feet away, directly before him.

His eyes began a search of the blackness for the face of Connor Beckett come to unleash him.

What caught his eye in the starlight, however, was the pair of yellow orbs, floating freely in the darkness, staring back at him. Then the low growl of the lone coyote grew louder and closer.

"Ah, Jesus, no. Not this."

He fought hard against his bindings, but they wouldn't budge. "Get outa here!" he shouted at the slinking coyote.

It was to no avail. The animal crept closer, showing no fear, probably emboldened by smelling the fear of his prey. Finally, the beast exhaled its hot breath as its fangs drew within inches of the man's face.

Then the coyote made its fatal lunge.

That sweet imagined scenario played over and over in Connor's brain. He could almost hear Charlie's screams.

That final scream, just before the coyote's teeth sank into his throat and silenced him, must have been loud and terrible, but Connor Beckett was nowhere near him to hear it.

Seeing coyote prints near the pond earlier that afternoon, he had concocted the plan of revenge that he then put into action.

Knowing that a coyote would come to quench its thirst sometime during the night, he imagined its joy upon its return to the watering hole to find a warm, rich meal for the easy taking.

Connor imagined Charlie's final seconds. How they might have played out for that murderer and rapist when he finally realized that Connor wasn't coming to his rescue. Or that God Himself had turned a deaf ear to the pleadings of an abysmal sinner.

What was that outlaw's final vision, Connor wondered. Was it the stricken look on the face of the innocent and terrified woman sprawled on the cabin's floor, staring up at him in horror and resignation as the light of life left her eyes? Or perhaps his last vision was that of the coyote's sharp teeth exposed in that vicious snarl, dripping drool, and drawing ever closer to him to tear into the soft and supple flesh of his exposed throat.

With the coyote's fangs sinking into his windpipe, Charlie's screams must have surely changed to gurgles. Then there came only silence. Connor Beckett could only imagine what the man's end might have been like. But it was a satisfying image.

Somewhere out in the desert, on the trail to that small canyon where Cutter Brown was expected to be hiding, Connor was seated by a warming campfire. For just a second another thought flashed through his mind, sweeping by so fast he almost didn't catch it. A faint smile lit his face as the light of the campfire danced in his eyes. Because somewhere out in the night, out in the desert — somewhere between Hell and breakfast — another small bit of revenge had been dispensed.

CHAPTER 12

Sarah's arms reached out to him. Her hands turned over slowly, opening as petals of a sweet flower to greet the nurturing sunlight. They inched ever closer to him until they lovingly embraced his face in a gentle caress. A warm smile graced her lips and her eyes brightened in joy.

Stepping even closer as he strode through the door of their cabin, she wrapped her arms around his neck. Her soft lips pressed against his in a passionate kiss. She was excited to have her husband back home.

She floated before his eyes as a gossamer vision of pure love and inspiration. Then her arms unclenched from his neck and her hands drummed gently against his chest as her eyes opened wide in dreamy surprise. Her beautiful smile grew wider as a silver hairbrush came into her view.

That wonderful expression of delighted astonishment filled his heart with joy.

Her hands pulled away from his body and clasped around the stem of the brush. She waltzed away from him to the rhythm of some unheard beat, caressing the brush to her bosom as she spun in tight circles.

Seconds later she was again before him, smiling brightly until two pairs of hands reached in from her sides and grabbed her arms. Her smile instantly disappeared, replaced by an expression first of surprise and then of a rising horror.

The hairbrush came free from her hands and was flung upward, spinning in slow motion, over and over until it disappeared from his view.

She was being violently and rapidly pulled away from him. Her hands thrust out toward him in a hoped-for connection with his, but it was no use. They were too far separated for such a touch to take place.

She freed herself with a yank of her arms and started for him. She made it only one step before she stopped abruptly and clutched at her breast. A trickle of blood oozed from between her fingers. Her eyes went vacant. Her head flopped backward. Her hands fell from her breast. He could see clearly now that she had been shot through the heart.

He tried to scream out, but he could not find his voice. His vision disappeared into a black void.

He awoke from the nightmare, panting like a dog.

He sat up and stared into the dying campfire. He wanted to cry, but as before, there were no tears within him. Instead, he looked up at the waxing moon and screamed out his unbridled rage.

Staring into the dancing flames of the re-stoked campfire, Connor tried to ignore the unceasing images of his terrible nightmare returning to his mind's eye over and over.

The blackness of the early morning hours was not helpful to him in reforming his thoughts. Besides those recurring images, there was nothing else for him to see except the last bit of the waxing moon finishing its fall into the horizon as if beckoning him toward his own end.

He sat staring into the abyss of blackness until the orange hint of the returning sun peeked over the horizon, giving hope to life for the return of the day.

With the coming morning, his vendetta was renewed. Night would return and with it more nightmares. He accepted both as his new way of life.

The day renewed the hate. The night renewed the fear — the fear that he might die before completing his mission of vengeance.

But with the hint of the new day came also a hint of regret. Connor now realized that he had killed three likely innocent Navajo braves. Of course, their guilt might be found elsewhere, involving another family. If so, their demise was a necessary dispensing of justice on behalf of some unknown others. No one out in this part of the country was completely innocent, he reasoned. His killing of them most likely saved the life of someone else. Through this bit of self-justification, he dismissed the incident from his mind. It was the best he could do; what was done was done.

He reset his mind to his purpose. Emptying some water into his coffeepot, he made himself the re-energizing brew. Soon he would be in the saddle, only a two-day ride to the canyon to slaughter everyone he could find there.

⸺⟩⟨⸻

Gerald Thompson closed the journal and again laid it down upon his lap. He sat quiet for a moment. Then he looked at Geronimo, who still sat by his fire, his back to the reporter.

"Was that the way of life out here back in those days? Conflicted and angry and filled with travail all the time?"

Geronimo did not turn his head.

"Life out in the desert has never been easy, Mister Thompson. Life anywhere, I think, is not easy for most people."

"But the crazy you spoke of. There is, I guess, a particular kind of crazy to try and live out here under such adverse conditions, at least back in them days… May I join you again by the fire?"

Geronimo nodded and Thompson joined him, dropping down onto his bottom next to the old chief.

"That is not the crazy I spoke of. The crazy is the thing that tries to find a place to live inside you, in the mind, the spirit. It is a demon. It is like a hand held up to block the sun from the eyes. One can see the light behind the blackness. You know there is light behind all the fear and hurt that stands before your eyes. You know safety is there in the light, but the light cannot warm you while you are hidden in the darkness. You are cold, and you are scared. But the light you see behind the darkness cannot save you until you remove the darkness in front of you. That is the crazy, Mister Thompson."

"I understand. It seems like Mister Beckett struggled with the right and wrong of what he was doin'. Is that the crazy?"

"Yes. That is the crazy. When you are filled with the crazy, no one can speak to you. You cannot hear their good words. No one can help you. The crazy blocks everything but what gave life to it in the first place. The demon is selfish. It wants only what is good for it, not you. And so it shields the light from you. It cares only that you live with it in the darkness."

"How do you fight against that, Geronimo? How do you win against the darkness?"

"When you learn that the demon is afraid to be alone in the darkness, then you understand that the light can break the demon's grasp upon you. But to learn this is not an easy thing to do. The demon tries very hard to keep your eyes down, so that all you see is the darkness. It lies to you and tries to make you believe that there is no light to save you. That your only choice is to fulfill the needs of the darkness."

"But isn't a bit of darkness a good thing sometimes?"

"Darkness is never a good thing. In the dark, a man stumbles over things in his path. It is only with light that he sees his path clearly and steps over those things that, if still hidden by the dark, would bring him to his face upon the path."

"What I meant is, sometimes doesn't the rage, the fear, the cold of the darkness give a man what he needs to bring about justice?"

"Justice is for those who walk in light. Revenge is all that those in darkness can see."

"Mister Beckett tried to justify the killing of those three Navajo braves. Was that the demon talkin'?"

"It was the demon. I have known this demon very well. I have fought with it many times. I have told myself that killing someone was wrong, but the demon told me it was right. It told me that to protect my people I had to kill anyone who might harm them. Its lies are strong. Its words feel good to the heart. It is hard to stop listening to the demon."

"Why didn't you keep Connor with you? Why did you let him go after those outlaws?"

"You have not heard my words. He was filled with the crazy, Mister Thompson. A man filled with the crazy has no ears to hear. He has no eyes to see. He has nothing in his spirit that can be saved. I could do nothing for him until the crazy was gone. Sometimes you cannot heal the crazy. Sometimes you can only heal what the crazy has left behind. Sometimes a person cannot be saved at all."

"But you saved him. How did you save Connor Beckett, Geronimo? How did you win over the demon?"

"It is in the story, Mister Thompson. You must finish the story to learn the answer to your questions."

"Then I'll get back to it."

Thompson reseated himself in the chair and opened the journal to where he had left off.

The sun blasted him with its furnace-like heat. The desert baked. The heat radiated up in waves in front of him, blurring the landscape.

He ignored every inconvenience. He ignored the press of the sun. He concentrated only on the vendetta surging through him, fully renewed, and his restored purpose. He had plenty of water. He had food enough. There was nothing to slow him down now. No men to torture to death. No more information needed. No one to track. He knew exactly where he was going, and nothing or no one was going to slow him down.

As the day reached into the late afternoon, he spied two riders coming toward him. There was nowhere to hide, no cover anywhere. He realized that if he saw them, then they saw him, too. He didn't know who they might be, but he eyed them warily as they neared.

He began formulating a plan to deal with them. Not knowing if they were just innocent cowboys heading somewhere or if they were men who harbored evil thoughts, he continued forward, considering his options carefully.

As they drew within a hundred yards, he raised his hand and waved at them. They waved back.

Good, he thought. *They seem friendly enough, to start with.* He wouldn't pull his rifle and gun them down without giving them a chance to prove their harmlessness.

Still cautious, however, Connor reached down and unhitched the leather thong over the hammer of his revolver and loosened the gun in the holster.

As they came within twenty yards of each other, Connor waved again and shouted his greeting.

"Howdy, fellas. It's sure good to see someone else out here. I feared I was completely alone."

"Howdy," yelled one of the men. "Yes, sir. If you're out in these parts alone, you're *really* alone. Where you headin'?"

They stopped just in front of each other.

"I was up in Tombstone," said Connor. "Headin' to Buenavista. How about you boys?"

Connor's eyes caught something, but he didn't let on that he'd seen it.

"We's lookin' for friends of ours. Maybe you seen 'em on yer journey."

"They got names?"

"Yeah. Charlie, Gabe, and Jeb."

"Three amigos, huh?"

"You got it."

"Well, just so happens I ran across three men a couple days ago. One of them was hurt real bad.

Didn't look like he was gonna make it. Could they be who you're lookin' for?"

"Yeah. They are. Where did ya run across 'em?"

"There's a spring about a day and half's ride due northwest from here. I met 'em there. We were sharin' the water. Had a nice chat with 'em."

"You don't say."

"Yes, sir. Say, fellas, them's good-lookin' horses you got there. I'm lookin' to replace this one when I get to Buenavista. Did you by chance get them there?"

"Nah. We picked 'em up along the way."

"Did ya, now? Well, they're great-lookin' horseflesh."

In a flash, Connor whipped out his revolver, cocked it, and aimed it directly at the men.

"Howdy, boys," he said with a smile. "I've been lookin' for you. That's my brand on your horses. In fact, those're my horses, you cowardly, murderin', rapin' sons-a-bitches."

"That's right," said Connor. "Jeb, Charlie, and Gabe are dead — dead as stones."

Connor picked up their holsters and revolvers and put them into his saddlebags without taking his eyes off both men, now hog-tied and laid out along the sand.

"So, boys, let me see if I got this right. You're Carl and you're Tannerfoot. What the hell kinda name is Tannerfoot?"

"It's my last name."

"Your last name, huh? Sure is unique, I'll give you that. Let me ask you, Tannerfoot, is that the name you want written on your headstone?"

"Why would you kill me? I ain't done nothin' to you."

"You weren't listenin' to me. I thought we covered that. You stole my horses. Did you miss that point?"

"Neither me or Carl had anythin' to do with stealin' your horses. We wasn't even at your ranch."

"I didn't say anythin' about havin' a ranch."

"I just assumed they come from a ranch."

"So that's gonna be your story? You weren't there?"

"We wasn't even close to a ranch."

"That's funny. Them three others said the very same thing. Well, two others, that is. I shot ol' Jeb dead right outa his saddle. Didn't get the chance to speak long with him, with all that coughin' up blood like he was doin'. But them other two swore up and down it weren't their idea. They insisted Cutter forced 'em to take part in them nefarious activities."

"We wasn't there. We met up with Cutter and the boys in Buenavista. He gave them horses to us there."

"There you go, then. You *are* a lyin' sumbitch. 'Cause when I asked you if you got them horses in Buenavista, you told me you didn't. You said you picked 'em up along the way."

"I meant we didn't *buy* 'em there."

"I'll say it again, Tannerfoot. You're a lyin' sumbitch. How 'bout you, Carl? You another lyin' sumbitch like Tannerfoot here?"

"He ain't lyin'. We wasn't up at your ranch. And we didn't have nothin' to do with any killin' neither."

"Killin'? Who said anythin' about killin'?"

"I mean we didn't have nothin'…"

"No! Wait! You said killin'. I didn't mention any killin'. How'd you know about the killins'?"

"I just assumed there was a killin' when the horses was stole."

"Darn it all. You *are* a lyin' sumbitch, too. I knew you were. I knew you both were liars. I just hate liars."

"Nice goin', Carl," said Tannerfoot.

"He bedeviled me, Hayden."

"Hayden Tannerfoot? Is that your name?"

"It is. What's wrong with it?"

"Nothin'. Nothin' at all. It's a fine name to die with."

"To hell with you, then, mister. Just kill us."

"What are you boys doin' out here?"

"We's goin' back for the money Charlie had in his saddlebags."

"You lyin' again?"

"No, sir. It's the truth. Charlie's got part of our share. He run off with it before we knew he had it."

"Is that right?"

"God's honest truth."

"Well, boys, you ain't gonna like what I have to say and I hate to break it to you like this, but you ain't gonna make it back to the money. Besides, I tossed it away. Probably spread all over the desert by now."

"What'd you do *that* for!"

"Tannerfoot, I'm here to tell you that Charlie and Gabe asked that very same question. Wanna guess at the answer I gave 'em?"

"No."

"No? You're not the least bit curious?"

"No. I expect I won't like the answer nohow."

"You're probably right about that. But heck, I'll tell you anyway. I told 'em they didn't need the money. Can't spend money in Hell."

"I don't like that answer. I told you I wouldn't."

"You did say that."

"Just do it. Go on. Kill us and be done with it."

"Yeah," said Carl. "Just do it."

"I was gonna plan somethin' horrid for you boys — a real torturous kinda death. But you know what?"

Connor waited for their answer, but they remained silent. Almost unaware of what they were asking Connor to do — almost oblivious to their own demise.

"But I just don't have time for you to die horrid-like. Just one question, fellas. Is Cutter in the canyon?"

"How'd you know about that?"

"Gabe told… No. That's not right, Carl. It was Charlie. Yes, sir. It was Charlie told me about the canyon. Yeah. Gabe was already dead from that rattlesnake I put in a sack over his head. Yep, that's right. It was Charlie told me. So, is that where Cutter is, Tannerfoot?"

"You put a *rattlesnake* in a *bag*?"

"I did, Hayden."

"And you put it over his head?"

"Yes, sir, I did. There was screamin' for a while, but after a time it got quiet. Tough way to go for ol' Gabe. So, is Cutter in the canyon, Carl?"

"You're a damn demon."

"I am. I am that. A demon and a whole bunch more'n that, Carl. Now answer the question, or I just might decide to take the time to give you the same kinda death."

"Yeah. He's there."

"Good, Carl. Now, fellas, another question. How many others he got there with 'im?"

"Three more," said Tannerfoot.

"Three more, huh? Four total? You lyin' again, Tannerfoot?"

"He ain't lyin'," said Carl. "Clay, Earle, and Flynn is with Cutter there."

"Who's Tugger and McCarthy?"

"Clay Tugger and Earle McCarthy," said Tannerfoot.

"Clay, Earle, and Flynn. Got it. Now, fellas, consider this a kindness."

Connor then shot both men between the eyes.

CHAPTER 13

The canyon, little more than a slight gouge in the otherwise flat but slightly sloping terrain, was created by erosion from heavy rains falling on the land over millennia. It wasn't all that deep, maybe fifty to sixty feet at the most. And it wasn't all that long, not much more than eight hundred to nine hundred feet.

The dry river wash that cut through the soft sandstone at the bottom of the canyon was only ten to fifteen feet at its widest point. The canyon was tiny compared to the larger canyons throughout the surrounding territory. So tiny, in fact, that no one had ever bothered to name it. To the locals it was just *the canyon*.

As canyons go, it was not, by any stretch of the imagination, of any other notable interest except for the campfire and the four men surrounding it near its end. With the canyon sharp and narrow, he heard the laughing and conversation as if he were only a few yards away.

After slipping out of the saddle about halfway through the canyon and pulling the rifle from its scabbard, he cocked it, and stepped lightly along the worn path through the dry wash, leading Tilly by her reins.

After a couple hundred feet of leading his horse along the wash, he dropped the reins to the sand. Tilly was trained to stay where the reins were, and he moved on alone, stepping in as much sand as he could to mask the sound of his footfalls.

Connor approached the men slowly and silently, checking again his revolver, assuring himself that it sat loosely within its holster — ready to be pulled to kill.

He heard the echo of laughter and the murmur of conversation louder as he drew closer. It didn't sound as if they were at all concerned for their safety.

This was going to be easier than he'd thought.

The conversation and laughter grew louder as he neared the campsite. He was as prepared as he could be for the fight he was certain would take place the moment he announced his presence.

It was several minutes more before he rounded the last turn in the trail and found himself staring at four men seated around the campfire. Only one man faced him, and he was drinking whiskey straight from the bottle. It looked as if he had been at it for some time. The other three had their backs to him. This was going to be so easy.

He smiled as he stepped out from the shadow.

"Don't move, boys, or you're dead."

The four men jolted with surprise, but hands lifted up and away from their revolvers. The three with their backs to him slowly turned toward him.

"Now, I just told you not to move and here you go movin'."

"You got us, mister. We ain't gonna give you no grief," said one of the men.

"Oh, I know that. You'd be foolish to do that. I mean, I can imagine how you're all wanted dead or alive somewhere. So it don't make sense to rile a man who's got the drop on ya, does it?"

"You here with a posse?" asked the same man.

"Now, would you be Clay or Earle or Flynn? Or maybe you're Cutter."

The man facing him, on the opposite side of the campfire, an ugly man with a large scar down the right side of his face; a flattened nose; thick, bushy eyebrows; and dark, sunken eyes, lowered his bottle of whiskey and straightened up. In a deep voice he spoke up.

"I'm Cutter. Who're you?"

"I might be one of the posse waitin' for you at the entrance to this canyon. Or I might be the man whose ranch you invaded, killed his family, and stole his horses. Or I might be just a guy from Buenavista who heard about some bank robbers with a price on their heads who come down from Tucson with bags of money. Tell me, Cutter. Which one do you think I am?"

"I don't know, but I think I'm gonna find out real soon."

"Oh, really? You see, ol' Tannerfoot told me who was here with ya. And darned if I don't count four of ya, just like he said."

The muzzle of a rifle slammed into his back.

"I guess ol' Tannerfoot forgot about me," came a deep voice from behind him.

Connor let his rifle slip out of his fingers and drop to the sand. "Yeah, I guess he did. Damn, this is gonna hurt."

"Not for long."

He heard the thud and felt the blow to the back of his head. A split second later everything went silent and dark.

━━━━◦◦◦◦◦◦◦━━━━

"Thinking less spares the brain," the fast-talking, high-pitched male voice said from somewhere unseen.

"Wha...?" Connor was groggy and uncertain about where he was.

"The brain. The brain. Spares the brain," answered the voice.

"I don't..."

"Thinking, you fool. Stop thinking. You'll wear out your brain thinking too much. Save some for later."

"Who...are...you?" said Connor, struggling for each word.

"Heneford. Barlow Brighton Heneford. You're lucky I found you out here. How'd you get to the canyon?"

"What?"

"I say, how'd you get out to the canyon?"

"Where am I?"

"Darn it all. I said you was out at the canyon. So I guess that means you're in the canyon. I told ya. You've been thinkin' too much. Far too much. Your brain is all worn out. Who tied you up like this, anyway?"

Six horses trotted into the campsite. One of them was Tilly, being led by her reins. The other horses were ridden by dirty, dust-covered men. They stopped in the midst of a cloud of dust swirling like a tornado.

They slipped out of their saddles and plopped onto the ground.

"Leave him be, Heneford," said Cutter.

"Oh, okay. Right, Mister Brown. He's with you, I take it?"

"He's mine!"

"Okay, okay. You should know, though, that he's been yellin' for his wife and kids, callin' out their names and such. Talkin' to 'em like they was right here. I told him they wasn't here, but he just kept talkin' like they was. I told him he's been thinkin' too much. He don't seem right. I believe he got knocked in the head."

"He did, you fool," said a big man, stepping forward. "I'm the one that knocked him in the head."

"Oh. Sorry, Owen. I didn't know that."

"What are you doin' here right now, Heneford?"

"You told me to meet you out here, Mister Brown. Here I am."

"At seven o'clock. You're early."

"Yes, sir. I don't like to be late."

"I like that. Did you bring it?"

"Yes, sir. One gallon of kerosene. Just like you wanted. It's tied over my saddle."

Heneford stared down at Connor, who had come around by then.

"So you got plans for this one, do ya, Mister Brown?"

That's what the kerosene's for."

"Oh dear, you gonna burn 'im, are ya?"

"Like chickens."

Barlow Heneford chuckled. Then he spoke to Connor.

"Mister Brown don't like chickens much. Says they're rats with feathers. Don't that just get ya to chucklin'? Rats with feathers."

Connor did not reply.

"Ya gonna torch him here?" asked Heneford.

"It's as good a place as any, I guess. Why?"

"No reason, Mister Brown. No reason at all. Just wonderin'. Can I stay and watch? I ain't never seen a man burn before."

"Heneford, sit him upright."

"Yes, sir."

Heneford tugged on Connor's shirt until he had him sitting up against a boulder.

"Like this, Mister Brown?"

"That'll do."

"May I ask what he did to rile ya so, Mister Brown?"

"He tracked us, Heneford. Eighty miles across this good-for-nothin' desert. He tracked us."

"That's bein' persistent. Why'd he track you all the way here? If you don't mind me askin'."

Cutter Brown turned and reached into one of his saddlebags and withdrew a small cloth doll.

"For this, I reckon. For this little bit of cloth, he come lookin' for us. Ain't that somethin'?"

Connor's eyes rolled back in his head and he screamed as loud as he could until a dusty boot slammed into his chin. His head snapped back against the boulder and he grimaced from the pain. His eyes danced in his head. He fell silent.

"Easy, Owen," said Cutter. "I don't want you to break his neck. I need him alive."

The big man stepped back.

"Would you like me to gag him, Mister Brown?"

"No, Heneford. I want to hear him scream real loud while he sizzles. A gag would just diminish the enjoyment."

Connor fought to regain his composure and senses. But the big man had scrambled his brains good with that kick. It was a slow process getting his senses back.

"So, horse man," said Cutter, looking straight into Connor's eyes, "you come all the way down here to do what? Kill me for what I did to your family? Is that why you're here? Did you really think it would be that easy to walk into my camp? Do they grow 'em that dumb up where you're from?"

"You're a rapin, murderin', cowardly sumbitch," said Connor coolly.

"Well, yeah, I am. But that ain't the worst of it. I'm a whole bunch nastier'n that."

Connor stared knives through Cutter Brown. Cutter smiled.

"I'm a man-burner, too. I'm a horse-burner. Hell, I'm an everything-burner. Lately, though, I've been partial to chicken burnin'. I just hate chickens. I don't know why, but I hate 'em. And you look like some kinda chicken to me. So, I'm gonna burn ya. Now, as for your wife. She was real pretty. And she was most...now, what's that word I'm lookin' for?"

"I believe the word you're lookin' for is *accommodatin'*, Cutter."

"That's it. Thank you, Earle. That's the word. Your two girls was so very accommodatin' to me and my boys. We was havin' such a good party with 'em, we just hated to leave. But you know, you just can't stay long in any one place when there's a posse lookin' for ya. I like this doll. I think I'm gonna keep it. It brings back good memories. I believe they call it, ah...ah...Earle, what's the correct word here?"

"Keepsake, Cutter."

"Thank you, Earle. That's it. It's a keepsake of my good times with your family."

"I'll kill you," said Connor between clenched teeth. "I swear it. Before I die, I'll kill you, Brown."

Cutter Brown picked up the tin pail of kerosene and shook it lightly. It was full. He smiled, then tugged on the stubborn cork. "I believe many would call that an empty threat, mister… Say, just what is your name, anyway? I like to know who it is that I'm about to burn to cinders."

"Connor Beckett's the name. But you don't need to remember it. 'Cause you ain't gonna live long enough for it to matter."

"Again, Connor Beckett, an empty threat. I ain't the one all tied up and about to get torched."

Cutter Brown wrenched the cork free just as a very large rock tumbled down off the cliff, making a loud racket as it rolled over other stones and bounced off the cliff's face on the way to the ground. It shattered as it struck the ground, sending stony shrapnel in all directions.

Chaos followed.

"Down here!" yelled Connor. "Cutter Brown is down here!"

Owen kicked him once more under the chin, in an effort to shut him up. Connor's eyes rolled in his head. A mist filled his brain. But his eyesight and brain remained able enough for him to distinguish a single arrow slice through the neck of the big man just before passing over once again into that land of blackness.

CHAPTER 14

It was the bouncing about that brought him around. As he regained consciousness, he felt himself draped over a saddle on his stomach. He was blinded by a bag over his head and he was gagged.

From the gait of the horse, he felt as if he was on Tilly. And although both his hands and feet were tied, he could move them about, so he knew he wasn't tied to the saddle or lashed to his horse in any other manner.

He thought about it a moment and realized that if he slipped down off the horse, whoever had him captive would have to stop to retrieve him. With bound feet he didn't expect to get far, but it would cause a delay in the procession. Maybe that might be enough. For what, he didn't know, but he felt that delaying anything was better than capitulation.

Well, he thought, if Cutter hadn't killed him by now, he must have other plans for him. And whatever that might be, maybe he could slow them down a mite for the pursuing posse sure to be after him and his gang, what was left of them anyway. Perhaps that's why they'd left the canyon in the first place. Perhaps the posse was closing in on them.

He made his decision. He stiffened his body and slid off the saddle, hit the ground, and fell over, striking his head on a large stone. His head began pounding again. Perhaps it wasn't the wisest move he could have made after all.

No words were spoken. From the sound of it, no one stopped. He lay there thinking that he might just be alone. Perhaps his captors had placed him at the end of their procession. Perhaps they hadn't realized he had fallen off his horse.

He listened hard. He heard nothing unusual. There was no conversation. No laughter. No sound but the wind.

Then he thought that he might be alone out here. That someone had laid him over his saddle and slapped Tilly's behind. He might be out in the desert completely alone.

New concerns filled his thoughts. He was tied up and alone in the desert. An abrupt vision of a hungry yellow-eyed coyote clamping its teeth upon his throat had him troubled and suddenly alert.

Then a blurry recollection visited him. He remembered the hard kick to his chin by that big man, Owen, back at the camp. But more than that, he recalled the arrow striking Owen in the neck just before the darkness came over him.

Apaches! That was Connor's next thought. Apaches had attacked Cutter in the canyon. That seemed logical, but why had they spared him?

Several other thoughts hitched themselves to his brain, but one became more important than all the others. He had to free himself.

His hands struggled against the bindings. They were tight. Too tight. Whoever tied him had done a good job.

He might be a free man again. But the bindings would have to come off if he was to enjoy his freedom. For now, he was going to enjoy his respite from captivity. He would figure out the why, who, and how later. Right now, he had to find a sharp rock to cut the bindings around his wrists. When truly free, He would set out again to pursue Cutter and his gang to a bloody end — either theirs or his.

That brief respite was summarily dashed when he felt muscular hands drop upon him and lift him high into the air only to once again land belly down over a saddle.

He felt several wraps of lashing going across his body. He wouldn't be allowed to slip off again.

"Wait!" he screamed through the gag.

But no one waited. Nor did anyone speak. He heard only heavy breathing.

"You sons-a-bitches!" he shouted in muffled words.

But no one responded.

And soon he was moving again.

The heat was nearly unbearable on his back. He was growing very thirsty. He tried to call out for water, but the gag was too big and too tight for him to form proper words.

He began struggling against his bindings. It was no use. His captors had done their job well.

After what seemed like hours, just when he thought he could take no more, the horse stopped. Hands undid the lashing and he was lifted off the horse. The muscles of his stomach were sore and bruised, making it difficult to breathe. At that moment, he didn't have the strength to fight.

The hands dropped him to the ground. His hands and feet were left bound, but his hood was lifted. The sudden flash of sunlight burned his eyes. He closed them and then opened them again a little at a time until they had adjusted.

Looking around, as far as he was able, he saw the Apache markings on the surrounding clothing.

"Not again," he mumbled.

He was once more the unintended guest of the Apache.

A long piece of cloth was wrapped around his head as a blindfold. He thought about struggling against it, but better judgment took hold of him.

What he saw briefly, though, were six braves. They were fierce-looking young men who neither smiled nor frowned.

After the blindfold, he could only listen to what was going on around him. Nothing, he concluded. Except for the occasional whistle of wind whipping by, there came no other sounds.

They sat, resting comfortably and silently. A brave brought over a waterskin. He yanked the gag from Connor's mouth and directed a steady stream of water into his mouth.

Connor cooperated fully, believing that any sign of rebellion would result in the water being taken away. And he was desperate for the water. The cloth gag had acted like a sponge, sucking nearly every drop of moisture from his mouth, so he was eager to drink his fill. He behaved himself and drank as much as he could, as fast as he could — as much as they allowed him, anyway.

Abruptly, the stream ceased and the skin was taken away, but he wanted more. "More water," he said. "I need more."

But the brave only grunted at him, replaced the gag, and walked away.

After nearly an hour of sitting in absolute silence, the braves replaced the bag over his head and lashed him to the saddle.

Within minutes, they were moving.

After what seemed like several more hours, they stopped once more. He was lifted down from the saddle, given water, and then immediately slapped back over the saddle, and they began to move.

After the passage of more time, Connor felt a coolness on his back. They had either gone into shade or the sun had dipped into the horizon and it was night.

After a short time more, Tilly stopped.

Hands once more lifted him down from the saddle and placed him on the ground. His hood and bindings were left in place.

He listened, but only one or two words were spoken. How could men come together and remain so silent, he wondered.

A while later, it was impossible to tell how long, hands reached in under the hood and removed the gag only long enough to stuff some food into his mouth and shoot a few streams of water into his throat. The gag was replaced and he was left alone.

He soon felt the warming of a nearby fire, and concluded that it was night after all and they were bedding down.

A blanket was spread out over him. The leeching sun had done its job on him, and he faded off into a deep, dreamless sleep.

The next day was the same as the day before. And the night much the same as the night before.

It was about mid-afternoon on the third day that things changed.

When Tilly stopped then and he was lifted down off the saddle, he heard conversation and some laughter, all of it coming from voices sounding like those of women and children.

Connor assumed by this that they had arrived at the main camp of the Apache. They had arrived and he was alive. He had no idea why, he was just glad to be off that saddle. His stomach was a mass of knots — painful knots and bruising.

The sack was abruptly removed from his head. He shut his eyes tight to avoid the pain of sudden light. Then, slowly, he opened them and found that he was surrounded by the entire encampment.

Every pair of eyes, forty or so, was fixed upon him. Once again, the faces showed little emotion. Just ambivalent stares and sullen expressions.

He heard a male voice behind him, but he couldn't get his head turned around enough to see who the voice belonged to.

A young maiden appeared before him carrying a tortilla-like shell stuffed with some kind of meat. Connor didn't object to whatever the meat might be. He was hungry and ate it gratefully from her fingers. He even, at one point, smiled up at her. And as strange as it might be, he received a smile in return.

Then she squirted several streams of cool water down his throat, patiently waiting until he swallowed all he could before sending another stream into his mouth.

She even waited until Connor's thirst had been completely satisfied before she stood up.

Before stepping away, she reached out and placed her right hand upon his left shoulder and lowered her eyes for a moment. Then she stepped away.

To his surprise, the Apache formed a line and each stepped forward and placed their right hand upon his left shoulder and bowed their heads before stepping away.

When the last person to do that moved out of his sight, he faced only a cloudless sky.

An instant later came a hovering shadow that remained for several seconds before Geronimo stepped into his field of vision. He kneeled down in front of Connor, reached out his thumbs, and lifted Connor's eyelids, inspecting his eyes.

"You are more polite now," Geronimo said. "And I see that the crazy inside of you is smaller. Is this true? Are you now not as crazy as before?"

Connor managed a small smile.

"Maybe a little."

Geronimo smiled in return.

"Maybe. Maybe soon we will speak as men."

"Okay."

Geronimo nodded, stood up, and stepped away. Then he stepped back in front of Connor.

"For now I shall call you Crazy-Eyes, until your heart changes and *all* the crazy is gone and I can call you by a better name. My hope is to change your name before it is too late."

Connor nodded his response.

Geronimo placed his right hand on top of Connor's head, mumbled some words in his native language, and then nodded.

"I must cover your Crazy-Eyes again so that you do not spread the crazy to my people."

He stood up and motioned to the brave holding a white flour sack. Seconds later the gag was replaced and the sack dropped back over his head.

Connor remained quiet and calm, although he did struggle a bit against his bindings, but more for comfort than to be freed.

He heard Geronimo speak some other words. The slight chuckles from the others all around him convinced him that Geronimo was, in some way, mocking him.

It was clear now that he was being kept alive for entertainment's sake — a kept buffoon for the tribe's sick amusement.

CHAPTER 15

After what he could only guess was several more hours, a soft hand slipped under the hood, lifting it only as far as it took for his gag to be removed. The same food as before, a soft tortilla filled with some kind of meat, was gently placed into his mouth. He chewed it fast and swallowed it. A few more pieces were pushed into his mouth. The hand feeding him seemed familiar and he concluded that it was the same squaw maiden who had fed him earlier.

After he swallowed the last piece, a carved wooden cup of fresh cool water was gently laid against his lips and tipped upwards. He drank the cup dry. The gag was immediately replaced without any words being exchanged. That suited him, for he was too exhausted by the heat to find voice to his many thoughts.

He sat as quiet and still as a rock, appreciating the fact that the savages were civilized enough to see that he was at least cared for. It was odd to him, though, for he had heard the horror stories of how captives were treated from those who were lucky enough to have escaped their Indian captors.

So far, they had not beaten or abused their buffoon in any way. Perhaps it was their way of ensuring their later entertainment. After all, a beaten and bruised clown tends to be less fun.

After some time he began to entertain different reasons for being gagged and hooded. Perhaps, he considered, it was done in an air of mistrust of all white men for their wickedness toward Indians. Or perhaps it was as Geronimo had said, to protect his people from the madness of a man who still lived within some kind of murderous rage that was obvious to anyone who looked into his eyes. Or perhaps it was simply an overabundance of caution on the part of Geronimo.

As Connor had remained quiet for some time, he was rewarded by their absence, left alone with his thoughts.

A great while passed. All was nearly silent except for a chuckle now and then, and the occasional distant voices speaking calmly. Other than that it seemed even the Apache were feeling the deleterious effects of the oppressive midday heat. Perhaps it was simply siesta time. Being hooded made it impossible to tell what was going on around him.

Realizing there was nothing more he could do in his condition, he lay back and soon drifted off to sleep.

He awoke abruptly, feeling out of sorts. The sun continued its assault upon him. When he tried to sit up, he became dizzy. The hood was now like an encasing oven, and his breathing became labored as his lungs could take in only scorching dry air. His muscles cramped. He felt suddenly nauseous. His heart began racing. He was now finding it even harder to breathe.

He heard woeful moaning nearby. At first he wondered who it might be. Possibly, he thought, someone was as sick as he. But to his startled amazement he soon realized that *he* was the source of the agonizing whimpers and moans. He was becoming delirious. His perception of reality faded in and out.

A hand reached under his hood and carefully lifted it off. His eyes focused upon a lovely vision of his wife smiling warmly at him.

"Connor," she said softly, "come back. Come back to where you belong, my love. You've been away too long now."

"I'll be there soon," he answered. "I'll be home soon. I promise. I'm on my way."

"You're too far away, darling. Come back."

"I'm on my way. I'll be there soon. Tell the children that their father will be home soon."

"Connor, you need to come back before you drift too far away."

"I'm coming, Sarah. Be patient."

Hands suddenly fell on each shoulder. In a second, he was being pulled away out of the sunlight and into darkness. He tried to struggle against their pull, but their grip upon him was too great. He slipped farther and farther away from his wife until all light disappeared and all that was left was black.

Just then another gentle hand reached up under the hood and rubbed across his cheek and then his forehead. Perspiration flooded out of his pores and gushed down his face.

He heard a woman's voice speak some words and then, fading in and out of consciousness, he heard Geronimo's terse reply. An instant later the hood was removed.

Through his blurred vision, he had great difficulty focusing on anything before him. All he could see were fuzzy forms moving about immediately in front of his face. Anything farther away was perceived only as a slight mass of haze.

As he teetered on the brink of blacking out, the fog lifted slightly from his eyes. Movements before him cleared, although he still could not distinguish anything with any exactness. Cool water then flowed over his head and down his chest. He discovered himself groaning again. He had no idea he was in the throes of severe heat exhaustion.

As another cup of cool water streamed off the back of his head and down his neck and spine, he moaned once more, this time with relief. It revived him a little. Several more cups of water were poured slowly over him. It felt wonderfully refreshing. He remained calm and still as the squaw then took a wet cloth and dabbed at his forehead and face.

His gag was removed, and a wooden water-filled cup was again placed against his lips. He drank this cup dry in seconds. He was given another, and that, too, he emptied quickly.

After some moments, clearer vision returned. The squaw's face was the first to come into focus. It was a stirring and delightful sight. She was young and extremely pretty, and she had a gentle, caring look about her.

The cool dampness of the cloth and his wet shirt against his parched skin were invigorating.

Connor could not help himself. A smile broke across his face. She smiled back at him. It was a kind smile.

Then Geronimo spoke and she abruptly moved away. A second later, it was the cracked and weathered face of the Apache chief before him.

He spoke some more words. The woman's hands reached for the gag.

"No. Please," Connor begged. "No more. Please."

The squaw's hand stopped. Geronimo's face then returned with his own gentle smile. "So, you are not so crazy now?"

"No, please," Connor said. "No more gag. I'll be quiet. I give you my word. No more hood, please. It's too hot for a hood."

"Maybe the crazy is passing from you. I am not yet certain. I hear now the voice of another thing, but as yet, I think, this thing still has no ears. Perhaps later, after I am certain that all the crazy is gone, we will speak together, you and I, as human beings."

He stood and spoke to three nearby braves. They rushed toward Connor and picked him up. They carried him to his horse and stood him up against it. His hat was pushed down onto his head as one of the braves drew a knife and severed the bonds around his feet. Then the other two lifted him into his saddle, keeping his hands tied behind his back.

A fourth brave, standing at Tilly's head, picked up the horse's reins and guided her along a high mountain trail. Within seconds the entire tribe was on its feet and moving south through an area he had never seen before.

As his head began to clear, new questions took the place of stale, stray thoughts, replacing the haze. *Had he lost his entertainment value? What was to happen to him now if the fun was over?*

Soon even newer, more serious questions took form in his brain. *Why was he still alive? Why hadn't Geronimo already had him skinned and his bloodied carcass tied to a stake as a midday meal for the ants and vultures? What true agenda was being hidden from him? Was he perhaps being kept as a hostage in the event they ran into the army?*

Too many questions without answers filled his head. And in this blasting furnace of desert heat, even his boiling anger and hate were now a mere simmer. Maintaining his desired level of hate was exhausting work for him. Even murderous thoughts of Cutter

Brown were fading. It seemed that the energy-sapping beating of the sun had a way of calming enraged spirits in wild men.

Night had fallen finally, and the desert cooled off quickly. Just like Tilly, Connor was hobbled with a few wraps of leather strips around his ankles. The saddle had been removed from Tilly's back and laid on the sand under Connor's back.

While the chattering squaws prepared the nightly meal, the braves sat around a good-sized fire, chatting themselves. Connor lay by himself in silence at the edge of the fire's warmth nearly seven feet from the braves, but within easy sight of them.

New and strangely different thoughts filled his head. As his eyes wandered over the encampment, he noticed how similar these people were to his own. They seemed a quiet people. They seemed not at all what the newspapers and army reports made them out to be — heartless and mindless savages.

From Connor's vantage point the children played the same way his own had played. They laughed and giggled. They raced about until one of the elders hushed them up.

The women seemed to get along wonderfully well. They kneaded the bit of flour they had, presumably taken from the raiding parties on the white settlers, into dough for their flat bread, all the while chitchatting as any women might do while preparing the nightly meal together.

The men sat around the fire talking about whatever it was that Apache men talked about. They appeared to be normal people doing what normal people do. If it weren't for the fact that they were being pursued by a determined (though inept) army, intending either their capture or their complete destruction, the scene might be from any Indian encampment he might find anywhere.

Then Connor noticed Geronimo sitting alone near a great rock and staring straight at him.

Connor returned his stare, absent the malice and anger of their initial meeting, now a look more of honest interest and intrigue. Still unsure of one another, neither man acknowledged the other man's stare.

Geronimo was approached by a squaw carrying food. Connor watched the chief take the food offered and begin eating. With each bite, Geronimo looked up into the sky, seeming to study the stars or giving thanks to some higher entity. Connor couldn't tell which it was, but the old man repeated this sequence until he finished his last bite.

Then the same young maiden who had attended to Connor earlier in the day walked over to him with a tanned animal skin that held his dinner. She knelt in front of him and without saying a word fed him the cut pieces of tortilla-like bread wrapped around meat, similar to his midday meal.

He smiled at her as if to thank her. She returned his smile as before. She then emptied a cup of water into his mouth.

He wanted to say something to her, but he didn't know what to say. Finally, he just found the simplest of words in his throat. "Thank you," he said.

She nodded as if she understood him. Then she placed her right hand on his left shoulder again. He still didn't understand its significance, but stayed still, recalling how everyone in the tribe had performed the ritual on him earlier. She then stood up and walked away.

As he turned his head back toward Geronimo, he found the old man staring at him again. They exchanged stares for several minutes. Finally, the chief stood up and walked directly toward him.

What does he want with me now? Connor thought.

CHAPTER 16

Geronimo squatted down in front of him and with both thumbs opened Connor's eyelids wide and stared into his eyes.

Connor objected to what was happening, but stayed calm. He vehemently did not want the gag and hood back in place should the old chief deem it necessary.

The chief stood up and stepped away, waving his hand toward someone Connor couldn't see.

From behind, the bag was dropped over his head once again. He wanted to protest, but feared the gag being stuffed into his mouth, so he remained quiet.

Blinded, he had a sense that someone now sat down in the sand before him. His ears strained to hear anything, and they did — the steady breathing of that someone who sat just in front of him.

"The crazy in you is becoming smaller," said a voice he immediately recognized as Geronimo's. "But the sack is necessary to protect me from the crazy that still remains within you."

Instead of trying to speak, Connor just listened.

"The crazy is still too strong to share words. Tonight you will think much. I know this. Perhaps tomorrow all the crazy will be gone. Maybe not. In the morning I will look again."

He heard Geronimo stand up, but he could not tell if the chief just stood there or had moved away.

Connor listened carefully for anything else he might recognize. There were no more sounds near him. He suddenly had a more immediate problem to deal with. He had to relieve his bladder. For a time he tried to hold it, but soon he was writhing about and apparently moaning enough that he soon felt hands upon him attempting to help him stand.

As he got to his feet, he felt hands loosening the bonds from around his ankles. And then he was led away.

They soon stopped walking. Familiar hands then unbuttoned his fly. There was no time for modesty or embarrassment. The moment he was positioned to relieve himself, he did.

When he finished, his fly was re-secured and he was led presumably back to where he had been sitting. He was helped down to a sitting position and his legs were re-tied.

Throughout the whole event, not a single word was exchanged. And he was glad of it. There was nothing more humiliating that he could think of, except perhaps what might happen tomorrow when the evacuation of his bowels became necessary. But that was tomorrow. He would worry about that necessity then.

Night had come.

A blanket was wrapped around him just in time for the onset of the chill of the nighttime desert.

He could only sit quietly and listen to the life happening all around him. The bag was left in place.

Periodically, the same hands appeared inside the bag and gave him water or wiped a wet cloth across his face.

He was kept as comfortable as could be expected for being a captive of the fierce Apaches.

As the night continued, he listened to the murmurings of the people who were gathered here. He heard life as he had lived it playing out around him. The Apaches laughed and talked. He heard tiny chuckles and louder laughs. He heard children playing and adults talking seriously. He did not, however, hear the voice of Geronimo.

As the night wore on, he soon heard the conversations die away until all was quiet. His eyes grew heavier until the blackness of sleep overcame any attempt to stay awake.

He was awakened by the same hands, small hands, which helped him to a sitting position.

He was fed and given water and then left alone again until a heavier presence was in front of him once more.

The bag was lifted from his head and he saw the figure of Geronimo standing before him.

The chief squatted and then reached out his hands and turned Connor's head from side to side, inspecting his ears.

"It seems you have ears now. I wonder if they can hear. Can you hear my words?"

Connor nodded.

"That is good."

Geronimo then used his thumbs again to inspect Connor's eyes.

"Can you see me?"

Connor nodded.

"That is good."

Geronimo sat down on the sand and stared at Connor for several quiet moments. And then he said, "Do you think it is possible that we can speak to one another as human beings?"

Connor wasn't sure what he was being asked. He didn't respond immediately.

Geronimo stared deeper into his eyes.

"I think you hear me. But I'm not certain that the crazy has left your being yet."

Geronimo reached out his right hand and laid his palm against Connor's forehead. The chief then closed his eyes and began mumbling some words Connor could not understand. It seemed as if the old Indian was praying over him.

This ceremony went on for several minutes, then Geronimo fell silent, opened his eyes, and placed his hand back in his lap.

"I have asked Usen to remove the crazy from you so that we might share words as human beings. But perhaps Usen cannot remove the crazy from your being. Perhaps only you can do that. I want to speak with you very much. So I hope the crazy will leave you soon."

Geronimo reached out and pulled the photograph from Connor's pocket. Connor was about to react, but thought better of it. After all, he thought, Geronimo had given it back to him earlier. If he didn't want Connor to have it, he would have held onto it then.

Geronimo stared at the picture again for several more quiet moments. Then he looked up into Connor's eyes.

"I know these people. I think they were your family. I have something to tell you about them. But the crazy must be gone from your being so that your ears can hear the truth of my words."

He put the photograph back in Connor's shirt pocket.

"I know that a great hot hate fills your heart. I understand this kind of hate. It used to live in my heart also. It is a bad hate. It is a hate that burns like fire. And I know the fire burns deep in you — in your heart. When the crazy in you is finally gone, then we can share words about this fire. And perhaps you will hear my words with a cooler heart. It will be good to speak then."

Geronimo stood up. Seconds later, the bag was put over his head again, he was mounted in his saddle, and the morning's procession began.

* * *

The evacuation that he had feared happened. But it was over quickly and he was cleaned up without discussion. The embarrassment of it all passed from his mind, though he couldn't help feeling like a babe who had been cleaned and swaddled.

Whoever this squaw was, she was gentle, understanding, and very kind. Connor's feelings about these people were in the throes of a great transition.

At times, he wondered for what nefarious reason he was still being kept a captive. But the longer he was with them, the less he found he was able to justify the wickedness of their actions. They cared for him with great regard for both his comfort and his health, despite his being a prisoner.

Perhaps that piece of leather he found in his cabin represented another truth not yet revealed. After all, Cutter Brown had already admitted to the torture and murder of his family. So why did he still not trust the Apache?

CHAPTER 17

Another day's march came to a conclusion and nighttime fell upon Connor once again.

He had been fed, given water, and positioned in a comfortable place. The sounds of the tribe filled his ears once more, sounds of families and friends interacting.

They seemed the ordinary sounds of any white family he had ever heard. Except for the language difference, he might just as well be sitting around a campfire of pioneers or settlers.

The heavy presence returned and the bag was lifted off his head. Geronimo sat before him again, staring into his eyes.

"I do not see the crazy in your eyes. Is the crazy gone?"

Connor nodded.

"Can we speak as human beings now?"

Connor nodded.

Geronimo gestured, and the brave that stood behind Connor as a guard left them to themselves.

"Do you wish a drink of water before we begin?"

"I would. Thank you."

"Thank you," said Geronimo. "Two words only, but they are kind words. Gratitude, I think, is always kind. I'm pleased that you could find some kindness. It means that you are no longer crazy, for if you still had the crazy within you, you could not say such kind words. Yes, I think the crazy is gone."

The squaw who had been his caregiver kneeled in front of him. She put a cup in front of his lips. He drank from the cup, his hands still bound behind him.

He finished drinking, and the cup was pulled away. He smiled at her.

"Thank you for the water."

She smiled as if she understood his words, then stood up and moved silently away.

"You rescued me from the Brown Gang. Why?"

"The men I sent were to watch you. But you were about to die. So they started a fight."

"Did they kill the leader?"

"No. They had many guns. There was much gunfire. Too much for my four braves."

"How did they rescue me?"

"They fired many arrows. The White-Eyes were afraid. They got on their horses and rode away very fast. One was killed."

"I saw him die. But the others got away?"

"My braves hit some of them with arrows, but they did not fall from their horses."

"So four got away?"

"That is the number I was told. One dead and four who rode away. But my braves got you and your horse."

"I would like to thank them for my rescue."

"Another time."

"Okay."

"Can we now speak of your family?" asked Geronimo.

"My family is dead. What is there to speak of?"

Geronimo studied Connor's eyes again.

"It is not polite to speak of the dead. So we will not speak of them. But I want to speak to you about your loss. You feel great hate for those who have killed your family. I understand this hate. I, too, was filled with hate when my family was murdered."

"Then you'll understand why I have to kill everyone involved."

"Before, in your crazy, you could not hear me. Perhaps you can now. We did not kill your family."

"I know."

"You know this?"

"Yes. White men, outlaws, they killed my family. They lied about it at first. But then they spoke the truth. I've killed five of them already."

Geronimo nodded.

"One who lies is of a low nature."

"One who murders innocent women and children is of a lower nature."

"To kill the innocent is of low nature. That is true. A low nature is born in the darkness. And only until light shines upon such a nature can it ever know anything but darkness."

"Then you, too, know the darkness within?"

"I know it. I know it too well. Such darkness lived in me for a very long time. It is not so dark now."

"Then release me and let me finish what I started. I need to find them murderin' sumbitches and slaughter them all."

"The need for revenge is still strong in you. I can see that."

"It is. And from the darkness I now live in, I will reach out of it with hate and annihilate them."

"You might die trying. I do not want you to die in the darkness of your hate."

"After I kill them all, it won't matter what happens to me. But between me and you, there is the matter of a torn piece of leather with your markin's on it."

"A piece of leather?"

"Yes. It shows me either you or your braves was at my cabin."

"And where is this piece of leather now?"

"It's in my saddlebag."

Geronimo turned and spoke to a nearby brave, who immediately searched the saddlebags and found the piece of leather. He placed it into Geronimo's hand. The chief studied it for a moment and then called out for one of the other braves. When he arrived, Geronimo handed him the piece of torn leather. The brave looked at it and then held it up to his own shirt. The piece fit perfectly.

They spoke in their language for a short time. Then, with a wave of his hand, Geronimo sent the brave away. He turned back to face Connor.

"It's true, then," said Connor. "Your people had something to do with my family."

"He is Stands Too Tall. He tore his shirt looking for things to take from your cabin. He had nothing to do with your people. They were already dead. But he is very much like you, Crazy-Eyes. His family was killed by White-Eyes."

"I guess he hates all White-Eyes now?

"No. He does not hate all White-Eyes."

"Did he get his revenge?"

"That is not for me to say. You must ask him."

"He speaks English?"

"Enough."

"Then I'll ask him. He at least must understand my hate."

"Perhaps. What are you called by your people, Crazy-Eyes?"

"Connor Beckett. That's who I am."

Geronimo nodded.

"The hate that burns in your heart once burned in my own heart, first for the Mexicans who killed my family and next for the White-Eyes who stole from us our home and our way of life. It was a hate that had burned too long, and I am growing older each day. The fire of that youthful hate has finally burned itself out, and I do not miss it. Only fear of not living free lives in my heart now. But struggling against my fear requires much from me that I do not seem to have anymore. To live at all, I think that soon I will have to lose my fear also."

"Well, sir, you have no need to fear me. You are not my enemy. I see that now."

"It is true I sent my braves to your cabin, but only for food and to steal your horses. But they returned to me and told me of what they had found in your cabin. The horses were gone also. Stands Too Tall told me the tracks of your horses were headed in this same direction. So I went to see for myself, and it was true. I chose to follow the tracks, hoping to catch up to the men and steal your horses from them — those who killed your family."

"I've been followin' those tracks."

"And we have watched you."

"So you got there after they were killed?"

"I have said this. I looked at your family to see if any life remained in them. But there was no life. They had gone to the next world."

"I need to find the outlaws that killed them. You, of all people, should understand my need to find them."

"I did not know who killed your family until the next day. I sent my braves to follow the horses. They returned and told me that there were eleven men and they had many guns. That they were in a great hurry and that they moved too fast for us. We have many old and many young. We could not do much to them. So I chose to let them go away from us. But then my braves saw you follow. You were filled with the crazy for blood. I thought it must be for your family, but then I saw the picture and I knew for certain."

"I believe you."

"I shall mourn with you for the loss of your family. I shall sing a song to their spirits that they may find an easy path to the next life."

"All the mournin' in me is done. I just want to kill the men that killed my family. I don't much care about nothin' else."

"The men you seek run for their lives. For now, we are also running for our lives. But one day we must stop running away. If we have the strength to stand and fight the Blue-Coats, we will. If we do not have the strength to fight, we will surrender. I do not want to surrender, but I want to live. I want to live not because my life is important to me. I want to live because the story of my life is important to me. If I die, who will tell my story? The White-Eyes? The White-Eyes lie. I do not want the story of my life to be told by those who lie. I want to tell my own story. I want to tell the great story of my people. I want to tell the truth about me and my people. So this is why I will surrender if I cannot outrun the Blue-Coats."

"I understand," said Connor, seeing this man and his people through continuously evolving eyes. "But I have to avenge my family. You should hear me. You should understand me."

"I understand, Connor Beckett, but do not let the hate inside you destroy you. Do not allow the crazy ones to destroy the calm of the sacred place within you."

"They already did. But I reckon I owe you an apology. I killed three braves back a while ago."

"They were not my people. They were Navajo. We avoid them when it is possible. You do not owe me anything."

"Why ain't you killed me yet? If you hate the White-Eye so much, why ain't I dead?"

"I do not hate white people. I do hate the army. At first, I thought you were a scout for the army. They are trying to find us now, but they are fools. They do not know where to look for us. I was going to have you killed. But then I thought you might follow those who killed that family. After I saw the picture, I saw myself in you. I felt your pain. I have felt it as strongly as you do for many years. I killed many Mexicans after my family was killed. I thought I might kill many more Mexicans before I die, for what they did."

"And have you?" asked Connor.

"When I was younger and I found my family dead at the hands of the Mexicans, a great flame of hate rose up inside me. It burned my heart. I felt the heat. And I wanted to cry hard so the tears would rain down on the flames and the fire would go out. But I knew that I could not cry hard enough to put out the fire. Still, though, I cried. I cried all the tears from my eyes until I had no more. And without the tears to stop the fire, I burned hotter. I hated more. I killed more Mexicans. But all the burning, all the hating, all the killing did not bring my family back to me. And now I grow older and weaker each day, still wishing to cry for the loss of my family. But my eyes remain dry. The fire of my revenge has become only ashes. And, I think, the hate is gone also."

"I hear you, but I'm not where you are. Hate still burns deep in my heart. The fire of my revenge burns hot."

"It takes great strength to carry hate, to keep the fire of revenge burning hot," said Geronimo. "When I was young, I did not feel the weight. I did not feel the heat of the fire of revenge. But I am old now. I no longer have the strength to carry such a burden. The great flame has quieted much. Only embers remain. And I know that even if I killed every Mexican on the earth, still it would not bring my murdered family back to me.

"And so I have laid my hate down in order to lighten my walk. I threw the ashes of my revenge into the wind so that they might fly far from me. I have found also that holding onto hate and anger is like stabbing a knife into my own heart and waiting for someone else to die. It is something only a fool would do."

Geronimo smiled.

"I was once that fool. I do not do foolish things like that anymore."

"Well, I ain't ready to let the hate and anger go just yet. And it may be foolish to do so, but I aim to kill 'em all before I die."

"Hear me," said Geronimo. "In time, death will come to us all. There is no need to run toward it."

"I ain't dead yet."

"I will die. I cannot escape my own death. You will die also. All people shall die. It has always been so, and it will always be so. But hear me. How we live is more important than how we die. It is not our death that we should fear, but the poor words spoken about our journey through this life after we are gone if we do not die well — with honor. How we are remembered, this is the important thing for any person. So I say again to you, how we live is more important than how we die, unless we live without honor."

"Them that killed my family live without honor now. I expect they'll die bein' the same. And I'll spit the name of my family into each one's face as he perishes."

"Hear me, Connor Beckett. I do not wish you to live with the hate you have now in your heart. It is not a good thing. It will eat your heart away until only a black hole remains."

"I have only my hate keepin' me alive. It's the only thing I own now," replied Connor, mournfully.

"Take care to keep only that which you truly wish to own," said Geronimo, "for that which you choose to own will own you also and you will have to live together for a long time. For your life, I hope you choose to live well. To live well, to live peacefully, you must empty your heart of all that is not needed for your journey on your sacred path."

"You sure ain't like how I saw you in my mind."

"How did you see me?"

"As a cutthroat, murderin' savage that kills anyone and everyone, just for the sake of killin'."

Geronimo nodded understandingly. "It is hard for men to know one another unless they speak face to face and see the one who lives behind the eyes. Many people say different things about me. They speak about me as if they know me. But they do not know me. How can one man speak truthfully of another unless he knows him? How can anyone judge the heart of another unless he has dressed himself within the same skin and heard the same heart beating? Do you have answers for this?"

"I reckon it's just the way of folks."

"It is philosophy," said Geronimo, striking a mock stately pose. "I was once told this by a White-Eye. Everyone said that he was a great and important person in his town. He wore new clothes. He ate good food. He was rich — very civilized. 'It is philosophy that separates us, you, the savage, and we, the civilized,' he said. 'But I do not understand this word,' I said to him. 'What does this word mean, *philosophy*?' He scratched his chin and took his coat lapels in his hands, raised his chin up high in a great noble manner, and said, 'Philosophy can be defined as a system of principles for guidance in practical affairs.' He was very proud of his words. It made him very happy to speak them. But I still did not understand. He then looked at me in a proud and high manner and said, 'The wisdom that guides civilized people through their daily affairs, my savage friend. That is philosophy.'"

Geronimo looked at Connor and smiled. "I hear this civilized man went crazy years later from his philosophy and ran around the town naked."

Connor chuckled. Geronimo smiled.

"But I thought about what he said," continued Geronimo. "He called me a savage and so I asked him, 'What is a savage?' He looked at me and smiled. 'Why, it is you, an uncivilized human being.' He called *me* uncivilized. I thought about this and then I asked him another question. 'What is uncivilized?' He said, 'Not yet civilized, lacking in culture or sophistication.'

"I also did not know this word, *sophistication*, but I grew tired of his words. I thought maybe philosophy is speaking great words that people do not understand. If this is so, then it all makes sense to me. Philosophy is speaking so that no one can understand you. I think maybe he was right. It *is* philosophy that separates us, for when I say 'You are a good person,' I mean you are good. When I say you are not a good person, I mean you are not good. When I speak in this manner to my people, they understand my meaning. Does this mean that I do not have philosophy?"

Connor sat stunned for several seconds. Geronimo stared at him. Connor then smiled.

"No. That is not what philosophy means."

"Can you tell me, then?"

"Philosophy describes a belief — a belief in how one lives their life. For example, if you believe that one should not kill another, that is a philosophy."

Geronimo smiled and nodded his head. "Now I understand. As I said before, it is more important how you live than how you die. This is my philosophy. Is this correct?"

"It is," Connor answered.

"Then I believe my people have great philosophy."

"I have a question," said Connor. "May I ask it?"

Geronimo nodded.

"If your philosophy is so great, wise, and wonderful, why hasn't it protected you from the pains inflicted by the White-Eye?"

"I have met now many white people. I like them very much. They are kind and generous. I have seen this. But the army is different. They lie. Their words have no honor. I do not think my philosophy is wrong. I say that the One God of the White-Eye made the White-Eye very strong. They come as many, like the blades of grass in a field. They have more guns and horses than the People have.

"My God is Usen. I once thought Usen and the One God of the White-Eye were the same. But I no longer think that is true. I believe they are different. I believe that Usen does not hear the People. That is why we are weak now."

"Perhaps His ears are plugged," said Connor.

"Perhaps it is our poor words that fail to reach His ears."

"Poor words? Your words are rich and they reach me okay, I reckon. No, perhaps you need to find a new Usen. This one doesn't seem to be listenin' or He's incapable of hearin'. Either way, He ain't doin' ya any good, seems to me."

"Crazy-Eyes —"

"My name is Connor Beckett, not Crazy-Eyes."

Geronimo leaned at the waist and looked deep into Connor Beckett's eyes.

"Are you certain? I think maybe the crazy is returning. Perhaps we should stop talking."

"No! No. I want to talk more. I'm not crazy, but you can call me Crazy-Eyes if you want to. I want to talk more."

Geronimo stared into Connor's eyes and then reached out and lifted his eyelids and peered deep into his them. He stared for several seconds, then nodded and leaned back.

"Perhaps I was wrong. Perhaps the crazy has not returned. We shall continue speaking as human beings. I speak my next words to your heart only, though. It seems your ears are not ready to hear well enough. But it will be good if you are able to hear my words with your ears wide open.

"You speak poorly of Usen. You think poorly of Usen. You find fault in the wisdom and judgment of Usen. But I ask you, what man can understand the mind of Usen? Who can say what He might think of *us*? Perhaps He looks down upon the People and sees our great failures. Perhaps it is *we* who have not honored Him in all things done. From where I sit, though, I see great dishonor in us all, red man and White-Eye alike. I think perhaps both of our people are worthy of grace and protection from Usen. But maybe not today. Maybe tomorrow, or maybe not. Maybe when the new moon comes again. Maybe not. It is for Usen to know. Not us, I think. It is philosophy."

"Perhaps you're right, but it changes nothing for me. I have no use for philosophy. My family is gone and I intend to kill every one of those animals, Usen willing or not."

"As I said, your ears are not ready to hear, but you are welcome to stay with us. I see the good in you, Connor Beckett, even if you do not yet see it in yourself. You and I have much in common."

"If you free me and my horse, I'll leave you in peace. I truly see that you are not my enemy."

"The true enemy is within you, Connor Beckett. You fight against yourself — you fight against your darker self."

"Then it's a fight I must endure. I will kill them men. The hate livin' inside me demands it."

Geronimo spoke some words to a brave. Immediately the brave drew his knife and cut Connor's bindings. As Connor rubbed his wrists, he remained sitting. He drew his legs up in front of him and then crossed them.

"I wish it were not so, Connor Beckett," said Geronimo. "Hate is powerful. It makes a man crazy."

He then smiled slyly. "I think maybe it is like love. Love makes a man crazy, too. But I think you know this. Love is a good crazy. I wish for you that. For me, I am glad that hate does not live within me anymore. But I must overcome my fear. I do not want to be crazy with fear."

Connor nodded. "Maybe one day I'll see the end of my hate, too. But for now, it's the only thing keeping me goin'."

"This talk has been good," said Geronimo. "Come now, gather around the fire with us and smoke tobacco."

Connor nodded.

CHAPTER 18

Connor sat alone on a large boulder overlooking an area unknown to him. He reasoned that they had crossed over into Mexico a few days ago. But wherever they were on the map, it had been years since he'd sat alone out under the stars this way — this peaceful, quiet, easy way.

He held a tin cup in his hand, filled with hot coffee. It was one of the little niceties he enjoyed at night, especially after a good, hard day's work, along with a good novel. The splash of whiskey made for a welcome touch against the chill of the star-filled sky. But he would not drink too much, feeling the way he did. He knew if he got drunk, the demon in him would be unleashed. So a splash was all he allowed himself.

He had been left alone with his thoughts since sunset. Earlier, everyone in camp had learned the reason why he had been tracking them. He was amazed at the outpouring of compassion shown by people who only days before he had considered heathen, murderous savages — people he thought completely incapable of gentleness and understanding.

After Geronimo had explained to the people the reason for Connor's presence, they all, young and old, walked up to him and laid a hand on his shoulder — a sign of respect and their special and personal acknowledgment of his pain and loss. And Connor understood that these were people who very much understood pain and loss. More than he could ever know or understand — more than he could ever wish to know or understand.

The more he looked around him, the more he realized something else astonishing. He again saw how similar they were to his own people. The women and children were cared for just like any white family would be. But they possessed something unique — a wonderfully distinctive and special camaraderie, unlike his own people. They lived together as virtually one very large family, each individual no more important than any other in the band, except for Geronimo, who often sat quietly alone — separate and filled with serious thoughts concerning the safety and fate of his people. Connor guessed it was a command issue and then recalled how, during the war, the officers had always sat separate from the enlisted men at night when the fighting was finished and everything had quieted down.

Connor had always been his own man, thought his own thoughts, made his own choices. That was why he bucked every call to action around him from the Confederates and joined the Union Army. Although he understood and respected what the other side fought for, it just seemed more right to him. His decision to join the Union Army led to strong arguments back home in his father's house near the Brazos.

But that war was over and a new one had begun for him. Somewhere out there in the dark were the few left of the band of raping, murdering men bedding down for the night with nary a thought in their heads for the family now resting in clay graves.

Connor's heart filled with an unquenchable anger and a seething hate for those men without conscience. Tomorrow he would ask Geronimo to let him go after them. For tonight, however, he would be thankful to be among a peaceful people.

He heard a rustle of gravel behind him. He turned and spotted Geronimo standing there.

"Can we sit and talk some more, Connor Beckett?"

"We certainly can. Would you like some coffee?"

"I would like that. It has been a long time since I had coffee. Do you have sugar? I like sugar."

"Yes, I do," said Connor reaching for the pot still warm next to the fire. Would you like a touch of this as well?" he said, holding up the bottle of whiskey.

"No. I drank it before. It burned my throat and made me crazy."

"Yeah. This stuff'll do that to a man."

Connor filled a second metal cup and stirred in some sugar. He handed it to Geronimo. The chief sipped it and then admired the cup.

"This is a good cup. Very strong. I like this cup."

"Then it's yours."

"I would like that. What can I give you in return?"

"My freedom is all I ask. Well, my horse and rig, too, if you will."

"I can give you your freedom. But I cannot give you your horse and saddle. They were always yours."

"Thank you. I'm much obliged."

"What were you thinking about before I came to you?"

"I was thinking about where those boys from the Brown Gang are hidin' out. I already killed five of 'em, but there's six more left, accordin' to the count your braves made when they first saw 'em. Wait! I remember one got an arrow through his neck. Must've been your braves that did it, comin' for me. So there's five left, I reckon. But there was only five men at the canyon, so that would be only ten total. I don't understand."

"My braves counted eleven. That is all I can say."

"There must be one missin', then."

Connor then thought a moment and then snapped his fingers.

"I forgot about Heneford. No, there has to be another fella that left the gang before they got to the canyon. I didn't get the impression Heneford ever rode with Cutter. He didn't look the saddle-tramp type. But I won't forget about the missin' man. I want to get after them tomorrow. I'll have to find Cutter's trail; he could be anywhere by now. But there is Heneford in Buenavista. He shouldn't be hard to find. I'll start with him."

"I have learned much from you, Connor Beckett. The learning has been good."

"Ain't nothin' anyone can learn from me, Geronimo."

"My name is Goyahkla, not Geronimo. Geronimo is the name given to me by the Mexicans as they attacked me and my people. I do not like the Mexicans. I do not like the name they gave me."

"Sorry," said Connor. "I meant no disrespect, Goyahkla."

"You see, I have learned something more from you, Connor Beckett."

"What's that?"

"I have learned that you are a respectful human being."

"I reckon I was once, at least. I don't know about now. Maybe I still am, but I don't have much to teach anyone anymore and I think I'm too old to learn anything new. I used to teach my son about things I thought were important for him to know. I guess now I ain't got no reason to teach or to learn."

"One can learn from everything and everyone if one just listens."

"I don't see how."

"In order to learn, you must talk with the true People."

"I ain't got much use for too many people right now, I reckon, true or not."

"Not the human people. The People. The true People."

"What true People are you talkin' about?"

"The Tree People, the Stone People, the Water People, the Mountain People, the Air People, and the Star People. Learn in the way they learn and you will grow wise."

"I don't understand anything you're sayin'," said Connor. "Water People? Tree People? I can't talk to water and trees. How can I talk to them?"

"It is best to speak first when you meet them, because they are usually very quiet and listening."

"I still don't understand."

"When the days of Mother Earth were fewer and Man was a new being, the Stone People remained silent. One day the New Man walked from the river to the mountains. In his wandering, he came upon a large rock. 'Do you speak?' the man asked the stone.

"'I speak only when I have something important to say,' the rock answered. 'Until then, I prefer to remain silent.'

"'Why do you remain silent?' asked the New Man.

"'It is easier to listen if I am silent.'

"'What do you listen for?'

"'I listen for those who are not silent, for those who do not wish to listen, for those who are lost in their own importance and do not wish to learn the truth.'

"'Why do you listen for them?'

"'To learn,' the stone answered.

"'What can you learn from people like that?'

"'The reason I should keep silent, listen, and learn.'"

Geronimo smiled.

Connor nodded his head. "Now I understand. Sounds a little like what my Pa told me when I was no higher than the knee of a grasshopper. He said, 'If you're jabberin' too much, you might not hear somethin' important said.' I guess that's what you're talkin' about, am I right?"

Geronimo smiled. "I like your words. They are simple. The words of both of us, I think, carry the same meaning to one who has ears to hear."

"I don't know any other way but simple. I'm not a complicated man."

"There is no need to be complicated, Connor Beckett. You do not need to complicate your life to accomplish your life."

"Wise words, Goyahkla. You sound a lot like my father. He was a Texas Ranger back in the day, but I've always seen him more as a philosopher."

"Does he have philosophy?"

Connor chuckled. "Yes, sir. He definitely has his philosophy."

"Why are you not with your father?"

"I reckon I had my own philosophy to explore."

Geronimo did not reply right away. Instead, he sipped his coffee and stared out into the night. Both men remained silent for several minutes, then Geronimo looked up into the starry sky.

"While I was walking through the mountains one day, I met a man who was writing words on a great stone. I asked him why he was doing that. He said it was not to educate the rock, for the Stone People had memory enough of us Human Beings already. 'The truth is,' he said, 'I need to write a story and I don't have any paper.'"

Connor thought a moment and then turned his head toward Geronimo. "I don't understand."

"Our reasons for doing something do not have to be complicated. The simple needs one has are reason enough for what needs to be done."

"Ahh, I see what you mean. Well, you're right. I have simple needs. I need to kill every one of those men that killed my family."

Geronimo nodded, but sat still and silent for a minute, his eyes turned downward tot the ground as if thinking deeply about some something important. After a time, he looked up at Connor.

"I will miss you, Connor Beckett. I will miss your coffee, too."

Connor smiled.

"On your next raiding party, don't forget the coffee."

Geronimo returned the smile.

"And the sugar."

"Yeah. And the sugar."

Connor fell into reflection for a few seconds before speaking again.

"I just hope I can pick up their tracks quick enough."

"I will say kind words to Usen for you."

"Thank you, Goyahkla. I owe you much."

"I look at you and I see myself as a young man. I have watched this sky for fifty-six years now. It never changes. It never grows old. But I grow old. My thinking has changed over the years." Geronimo stretched out his arms and yawned wide for almost ten full seconds. He then looked at Connor and smiled. Goyahkla means "The One Who Yawns."

"I know. I learned that in the newspaper."

"Who writes about me?"

"Newspaper reporters, book authors. You're famous."

Geronimo thought for a moment.

"I'm tired."

"Even the famous grow tired," said Connor with a smile.

Geronimo returned the smile.

"I shall sleep and dream of one day being like those who travel about among the stars in their bright lights. Then, I think, I will be more famous."

"I don't understand," said Connor, intrigued but confused.

"You have not yet met the Star People. They are not like us, but they have helped my people many times. Sometimes after the army surrounds us, when they come to capture us, we are not there. It is because the Star People come and lift us up into the sky, into their light, and move us. We laugh at the soldiers. It is a good trick to play on the army. It makes them crazy."

"I have no idea what you're talkin' about."

Geronimo stood up and patted Connor on the shoulder. "One day you may meet them. If you do, it would be wise to be like the Stone People and remain quiet and listen. You will learn much."

He turned and walked away. After a few steps, he stopped and without turning back toward Connor he said, "I hope you lose the hate and the vengeance in your heart before it is too late, Connor Beckett. They are both heavy burdens for any man to carry."

Geronimo then walked away and Connor returned to staring out over the dark valley, ruminating on the words of the Apache chief.

CHAPTER 19

The first waves of morning light splashed over Connor Beckett, still sitting next to his blazing campfire.

"You have been here all night?" a voice behind him asked.

Connor turned to see Geronimo walking up to him. He carried Connor's revolver and gun belt.

"I have."

"Do you have more coffee?"

"I do. Join me, please."

Geronimo handed the rig to Connor.

"Is there trust now between us?" asked Connor.

"There is the need for coffee," said Geronimo with a smile. "The other guns are on your horse."

Connor took hold of his rig and set it off to the side.

"I have coffee. And I have sugar."

"Then it is a good trade."

"Indeed it is."

Geronimo sat down and handed Connor the tin cup he had received from him the night before.

Connor filled the cup and handed it back. The aroma of the coffee wafted over to Geronimo and he breathed it in.

"The smell of the coffee is good. I like sugar."

"Yeah. You said that."

Connor spooned in sugar in the amount he knew Geronimo liked, stirred it a few times, and then watched as the old chief sipped.

Geronimo smiled.

"I tell you again, I will miss you when you go, Connor Beckett, but I will miss the coffee, too. Maybe I will miss the sugar the most."

Connor chuckled.

"You won't miss anything. I've decided to stay with you for a while longer."

"You will not hunt the men who killed your family?"

"I will, but I would like to spend a few more days with you until we get deeper in the Sonoran mountains. If that would be okay with you. That's where we are, right? Deep in Mexico?"

"We are in Mexico. You are welcome to stay with us. But what of your great hate? What of your terrible vengeance?"

"The hate is still great, my need for vengeance still terrible. But all that can wait."

Geronimo nodded.

"It is good to keep hate and revenge waiting. They are like old men. They tire easily."

Connor nodded with a smile.

"When do we move next?" he asked.

"We wait now."

"Why?"

"We wait for those sent for supplies to return."

"What kind of supplies? You mean food and such?"

"Yes."

"Do you trade for the supplies?"

"They are Mexicans. I will not trade with Mexicans. I take from them."

"A raiding party, then?"

"Yes. There is a small village nearby. They have gone there to find what we need."

"I see. When are the raiders expected to return?"

"Two days ago."

"Are you worried about them?"

"I do not think it is a good sign."

"How about if I go lookin' for 'em?"

"It is too dangerous. All about, there are banditos who hate the White-Eye more than they hate the Apache."

"I recall reading about that. Is there anything I can do to help?"

"Make more coffee. It is good for me to sit and speak with you. It cures my mind of the infection of leadership."

"I can only imagine. What worries you most?"

"Keeping the trust of my people worries me most."

"You're a good man. I think they trust you."

"The good ask for trust. But so does evil."

"I don't trust evil."

"But what if evil comes wearing the headdress of good? How do you know that it is evil before it is too late?"

"I don't know."

"And that is what worries me. The things I do now. The running. The hiding from the Blue-Coats. Is it for a good reason or an evil reason? Is it for my people that I keep them here, or is it for my selfish fear of living on the reservation as a prisoner?"

"Whew! Those are questions of principle, I think."

"What is principle?"

"That's a tough question to answer. But I would say it is like a philosophy. In your case, I'd say a principle is a fundamental personal belief. A rule for proper conduct. A matter of personal moral ethics. A stand made and based upon the rules of proper etiquette."

"All these words are strange to me, Connor Beckett."

"How about this, then? A principle is a personal rule for what a person believes is right and proper."

"Yes. I understand these words. I like these words. A belief in what is right and proper. Yes, that is my principle. And it is a philosophy, yes?"

"Very similar. When you communicate with the army next, tell them that it is your belief that you should not live on a reservation, as a matter of principle."

"It is your belief…"

"No. You say this: 'It is my belief that I should not live on a reservation, as a matter of principle.'"

Geronimo repeated the sentence several times and then smiled.

"I think it is the coffee, the sugar, and the good talk here that turns my worries to mist."

"Good."

"I will tell this to my people later. I hope that they understand that we run and hide because of principle."

"I hope so, too, Goyahkla."

It was later in the morning when Connor noticed the commotion on the far side of the encampment. Everyone was scurrying about in chaotic fashion. Voices were growing in alarm. From what Connor could gather, someone was approaching the campsite and it had everyone upset.

Connor grabbed his rifle from its scabbard on Tilly's saddle. He moved toward the mass of gathering people. Geronimo stood in front and stared down the trail.

Connor worked his way up next to Geronimo and saw the approach of five horses. Two carried riders upright. One carried a body laid across it. Two others were laden with supplies lashed to them.

"The supply party?" asked Connor.

Geronimo nodded his reply.

"One man is down," remarked Connor.

"Yes. Tonight many tears will fall. There will be much shouting and arguing. There will be many questions asked of me for which I will not have answers. It will not be a good night."

"I'm so sorry."

"I am sorry also."

"But you have principle to help you."

"Yes. I have principle. I have philosophy. But tonight a woman does not have her man. Tonight, children do not have a father. What will principle and philosophy mean to them?"

Connor bowed his head.

"I don't know, my friend. Not much, I reckon."

"Perhaps tonight, Connor Beckett, I will need much coffee and sugar. Perhaps tonight we will need to talk together until the stars are gone and the sun returns to its place in the sky again."

Connor nodded.

"Perhaps."

While the women prepared the body of the slain brave with great lamentation, the men sat and talked about what was to come for them. While the women shed tears, the men shouted in a heated discussion.

Not being a part of the tribe, Connor removed himself to a place far outside the circle.

He could see the women performing their ritualistic duties. He could hear their required wails of torment and grief. He heard the shouts of the men and witnessed the wild gestures of flailing hands. He understood no words spoken, of course, but he thoroughly understood their meaning.

As evening approached, the men's shouting and arguing continued. Then there was a funeral ceremony for the dead brave.

They laid him out on the ground, cleaned and dressed in his best clothing. They gathered his every possession and laid them out on his body and then wrapped it in furs and cloth. They danced around the fire and sang the praises of the brave warrior as they announced to the next world the coming of a good man. Geronimo spoke the expected words of the tribe's holy man. Then a selected group of warriors carried his body out into the darkness.

Sometime later, the burial party returned. Nothing more was said or done regarding the dead man. Life, such as it was for the tribe, returned to as near normal as was possible under the circumstances.

Connor sat alone for another hour. Geronimo sat alone next to the fire some distance away.

The discussions and arguments had been exhausted. The council members had returned to their families and all was silent throughout the camp.

Yet Connor studied the wilted shoulders of the chief as he sat thinking about what Connor could only guess were very weighty issues — issues of security and safety and of a life even more uncertain than before the return of the supply party.

Connor had made more coffee in anticipation of a continued conversation with Geronimo, but it now sat cold within the pot next to the small warming fire in front of Connor.

From behind Geronimo, Connor spotted an Indian brave step out from his lodge and walk past Geronimo without any words.

The brave walked toward Connor and sat down across from the fire. He remained silent, staring into the flames.

Connor did not know if he should speak or remain silent, but he decided to be like the Stone People and let the brave begin speaking first, if he was going to speak at all.

After several minutes of silence, the brave looked up into Connor's eyes.

"I am Stands Too Tall. You are Connor Beckett. Tomorrow will be hotter than today, I think."

Connor smiled inwardly at the thought of how similarly most people began conversations with strangers. It was always safe, he guessed, to speak of the weather.

"Yes. I reckon it will. Does it rain much here?"

"Not now. After more moons, it will rain much. We will share words now."

"You speak English, too. Do many others speak as you do?"

"No. Only Goyahkla and I speak language of White-Eye."

"Where did you learn to speak the language of the White-Eye?"

"I speak it. That is enough for now."

"Okay. Yes. Your name," said Connor. "Why are you called Stands Too Tall?"

"When I very young, Pawnee attack our village. I stand up behind big log. Pawnee shoot arrow at me. It go across my head. It cut me, but that is all. After fight, Mangas Coloradas, chief then, called me to his side and told me I lucky. I now Stands Too Tall."

Connor burst out laughing. The Indian remained stoic for several seconds, but then a slight smile played across his face. Then Stands Too Tall leaned over and parted his hair with his hands. Connor saw the scar left by the arrow. He laughed even harder for a minute before stopping.

He wiped his eyes dry, then realized that he had not laughed like that in a long time. It felt good to laugh. He had missed it very much and hadn't noticed until that moment.

CHAPTER 20

With the morning meal completed and everything packed and readied for a day's march, the camp formed a line and moved out through the mountains.

It was about noon that the formation reached a small summit from which they looked down upon the shattered remains of an Indian village below.

To Connor, it appeared that fighting had ceased only a few hours before, for smoke still trailed upward from several scattered fires throughout the small village.

Stands Too Tall rode up next to Connor and stopped.

"This happened today," said Connor. "Earlier this morning is my guess."

"Yes. They come from darkness."

"They attacked before dawn, you're sayin?"

"Yes."

"Who did this?"

"We know soon."

Stands Too Tall heeled his horse forward and Connor followed.

As they entered the village, the slaughter became apparent. Bodies were scattered throughout the village. The loss of life was extreme.

Dismounted and now walking among the dead, Connor saw the hideous reality: every head had been scalped.

Stands Too Tall walked over to where Connor was staring down at one of the corpses.

"They Yaqui," the brave said. "They all shot. No arrows. And they all scalped. Mexicans. For Yaqui hair."

"Mexican scalp hunters?! Is that what you're telling me? They were killed for the bounty on their *hair*?"

Stands Too Tall nodded.

"I couldn't do that. Not even for hate's sake."

"You not Mexican."

"Mexicans aren't the only scalp takers I've known."

"They Mexican here."

Connor pulled on Tilly's reins and walked around the village, viewing more bodies until one in particular drew his attention.

A young boy lay under that of a woman Connor assumed was his mother. The child had been scalped as well.

Sudden emotion slammed him to his knees, and tears he had thought were nonexistent gushed from his eyes. He pulled the body of the boy out from under the woman and cradled it in his arms as he sobbed.

Stands Too Tall walked over to where Connor sat on the ground lamenting the child's passing. He stood still and silent. Within minutes, most of the Apache had surrounded him with sullen expressions.

A small group of survivors — eight children, two men, and two women — stepped out from behind some distant large boulders and walked slowly toward the Apache.

The Apache separated in waves as the Yaqui made their way to the sobbing white man cradling the child.

Everyone stood mesmerized by the white man's grief over the body of an Indian child. But they let him grieve for another fifteen minutes before Geronimo stepped forward and put his hand on Connor's shoulder.

Connor looked up at Geronimo.

"He's about my son's age," said Connor mournfully. "He could be my own son."

"His people will see to his spirit now, Connor Beckett. It is not for you to grieve any longer."

Connor realized that his grief was usurping the right of the Yaqui people to grieve in the way that was their custom.

He surrendered the body of the boy to the two Yaqui men. They nodded politely to him, a thank-you for sharing their own grief, and then took the boy's body away.

Connor wiped his eyes dry and then understanding flashed through his mind. Although there was honest grief felt for the young Indian boy, they were more truly the tears for his own family that had never found their way out of him. Because he had been so gummed up with hate and anger and revenge, the tears could not find an exit. Instead, they had been forced to remain within, lingering and fermenting into a bitter liquor of detestable spite.

The rest of the day, until nightfall, Connor stayed alone and chose not to converse with anyone — even Geronimo, who had tried on two separate occasions to console him with soft, well-chosen words. All he received from Connor Beckett was an empty stare and no acknowledgment of his presence.

Connor sat alone, without a comforting fire to warm him in the chill of the high desert night. He seemed impervious to the cold. He just sat and stared into the blackness at something only he could see.

An armful of wood fell in front of him. He barely noticed. Then a lighted splinter of wood was thrust into the heart of the pile. The dried wood responded immediately and flames leapt into the air.

Geronimo sat down next to Connor, but said nothing.

After a while, Connor sensed that he was not alone. His eyes very slowly moved from the blackness and found Geronimo's.

"I didn't cry when my family was killed."

"It is good now and then to cry. Tears wash the spirit."

"I don't know how clean my spirit is. But I think I needed to grieve for my family."

"I cried for my family, too. It was good, but I think sometimes I need to cry more."

Connor nodded and then fell silent for a long time. Geronimo let the silence stand. Finally, Connor looked at Geronimo again and said, "*The good Lord owes me an explanation for the things that happened in my life.*"

"Why did you say that?" asked Geronimo.

"It's something I heard Wyatt Earp say. You know who Wyatt Earp is?"

Geronimo nodded. "I have heard his name."

"In fact, I heard him say it more than a few times in Tombstone. The last time I heard him speak those words was after his brother Morgan was murdered. It was the next day, while he drank a cup of coffee. He spoke them very softly. He didn't speak them to anyone in particular, but I heard him."

"Why did he say that?"

"I've been askin' myself that same question for more than a little while."

"Have you found the answer?"

"I think sometimes we get lost on our path," said Connor. "When we do, we start lookin' for direction in our lives — a divine purpose for what we are doing, where we are going, and why we are here at all in the first place. We start lookin' for someone outside ourselves that we think is in charge of how our life is to go. Maybe it's simply that we get tired of bein' responsible for everything we do and say. Maybe we need to blame someone else for what problems come at us because we don't want to admit that we've made the wrong choices and brought those problems to us. Maybe there are some that don't never take responsibility for their own lives and they end up blamin' someone else for all their problems."

"Mouse and Coyote were facing each other in battle," said Geronimo. "Mouse was very near a hole in the ground where he could have easily escaped from the teeth of Coyote. But Mouse chose to stand his ground and fight instead. Coyote ate Mouse."

Connor nodded but held his words.

"There is a consequence to every choice we will ever make in our lives," added Geronimo.

"Do they always have to be so hard?"

"Some consequences are greater than others, but all choices must have consequences. We do not always know which they will be. Still, we must find the courage to choose. And then we must be prepared for what follows. It is the way it will always be, I think."

"I'm prepared for what comes at me. I deserve it all. I failed my family. I failed myself. I am weak."

"It is not about the thing that comes to us while walking on our sacred path," said Geronimo. "It is how we choose to greet it when it arrives."

"I understand," said Connor, "but I feel too weak to stand and greet it. And I know I can't stand against it anymore."

"One day," said Geronimo, "Coyote chased Raccoon for his dinner. Raccoon climbed a tree and sat on a branch staring down at Coyote.

"'You are powerful, Coyote,' laughed Raccoon, 'but I sit here and mock you now.'

"Coyote looked up at Raccoon and said, 'It is not you who mocks me and makes my belly rumble. It is the tree that mocks me, for if you were not on that branch, my belly would not rumble so loud.'

"Raccoon laughed harder, until the branch broke.

"Coyote slept well that night with a quiet belly."

Connor smiled in understanding and nodded, but held his words within him.

Geronimo shook his head slowly. "The weak can only mock the powerful for so long. We cannot outrun the Blue-Coats forever."

Connor nodded once more.

"And you, Connor Beckett. You cannot outrun yourself for much longer either. Soon it will be your turn to face yourself and decide what the rest of your life will be. But I think you will do well. You are not weak, as you say you are. You are very strong. Your head and your heart are strong. It is for you to believe, though."

"But am I? Am I really strong enough?"

Geronimo pointed to a piñon tree. It was terribly deformed, with many broken branches lying on the ground at its base. It barely looked like a tree at all. But it seemed to defy all the losses of its branches and refused to bow before the wind that had howled against it.

"Which is stronger, Connor Beckett, a tree or the grass?" asked Geronimo.

"The tree, of course," answered Connor.

"Look there. The tree has stood in battle against the wind for a long time. See how it is broken. It will soon rot away until there is nothing left of it — nothing left to show that it ever once stood. Look at the grass. It is everywhere. It is here because it bends with the wind. The grass will be here always. That is the power of true strength."

"But the tree still stands," said Connor. "It is wounded, but it still stands. And it is alive. And it still battles against the wind."

"It is already dead. But it refuses the call to the next world. That is why it still stands."

"Then maybe I should ask it how I might avoid my own call to the next world until I've killed the Brown Gang."

"Seek no answers from the dead," said Geronimo. "The dead know nothing to help the living. They do not know of good and evil, of right and wrong, of honor and disgrace. They know only the blackness of their own eternity."

"Again, though. It still stands despite itself bein' already dead and called to its eternity. Perhaps today it has some advice for me on how I might do the same. At least until I finish my task."

"Never seek the dead for the day's advice," said Geronimo, "for they can only speak of forever."

"You're a great man, Goyahkla. You lead your people with strong honor, with good reason, and just principle. I believe they will say great things about you in the years to come."

"There was once a man," said Geronimo, "who spoke loudly about his great skill as a bird hunter. One day he hunted a bird in a tree. He approached the tree quietly and readied his bow. But he was bitten by a snake in the grass and he died. And when the bird landed on the hunter to peck at his eyes, the snake bit the bird and it died. The snake did not speak loudly of his great skill as a bird hunter. Instead, he quietly enjoyed a good meal."

"So you choose to be the snake?"

"No! But I also choose not to be the man who speaks too loudly anymore. It is not good to speak too loudly. The army does not like an Indian to speak too loudly. It frightens them. But I have spoken loudly already. I cannot take it back. Now I must battle against their fear also."

"You are a man of courage, Goyahkla."

"I wish it were not so. Courage gets you nothing but remembered."

Connor chuckled. "It takes great courage to shout out your love for your people. But I think vengeance and fear sometimes speak louder."

"Louder, but not always better, Connor Beckett. And I think nothing is ever certain during times of vengeance except vengeance itself. I was once vengeance. I was once hate. I was once all things dark and terrible. And I would shout about it very loud for all to hear, thinking that such a loud voice would make them fear me and leave me alone. See my reward for my loud voice. Now it is *I* who feel the fear. And it is *I* who now speaks only in whispers, fearing that the army still might hear me, find me — capture me."

"There is still time, my friend. Things can change. There will always be opportunities for a man as wise as you. You just need to give it some more time, I think."

"Some say that time is an ever-spinning wheel, that chances missed will return again. Others say that time is like a river that passes by quickly, and that any chances missed will be lost forever."

"What do *you* say?"

"I say that you should take great care to use the time you have wisely in case time is like a river."

"I don't think you missed many chances, Goyahkla. And I think you have a divine purpose within you. I think it guides you in all things. I think you know what needs to be known. I don't believe your Usen withholds much from you."

"Sometimes all that could be known is withheld from us for something other than divine purpose."

"If it's evil, I suppose so, but I think history judges us differently than how we might ever judge ourselves. I think it will be remembered how much you loved your people."

"Your words lift me up out of the depths of my own madness. You gave me strength again to find a good purpose. You freed me from the sting of loss and fear. Such acts now bind me to devotion. And they shall never be forgotten no matter where I live. You are a good man."

"There is a flaw in your thinkin', Goyahkla. Your flaw is your belief in me, that I have any goodness still living within my breast — that there ever *was* anything good in me. I fear I will yet disappoint you. But I will tell you this. I gave thought only to annihilate. I believed it my right and duty to do so. But, like you, it is I who is destroyed — fated to a disastrous end, lost to life itself."

"I believe life contains everything — everything we will ever need to fully live our lives. But with that given comes a great responsibility to live wisely."

"I'm afraid I have fallen far short of that wisdom. I don't even know if it will ever be possible to find the wisdom I need."

Geronimo sat very still and quiet for some time before looking up into Connor's eyes again.

"One should always sit in the center, so that one will be always at the center of all things. Not because you are more important, but because when one is at the center of all things, then one is surrounded by all things. And if one is surrounded by all things, then all things are within one's grasp. And if one might grasp all things, then all things are possible."

Connor nodded.

"Sit in the center, Connor Beckett. Sit in the center and touch all things. Then see what might be possible for you."

"Even if I find the center, could I ever choose correctly again?"

"Answer this for me. Usen gave us the freedom to choose what to think, see, hear, feel, and experience all the time we walk through our lives — to make the choices we need to live as well as we can. It is not right that the Blue-Coats take our choices away from us. So, while I can, what choice do I make for my people? Do I choose life on the reservation or do I choose to fight on?"

"Choose life, Goyahkla. Choose life so that you might live to tell your story and the glorious story of your people."

The old chief smiled.

"And you asked me if you could ever choose correctly again."

Connor smiled and nodded.

CHAPTER 21

"There is a conscience to consequence. There is a consequence to conscience," said Connor.

"What do those words mean?" asked Geronimo.

"Try this. There is a principle to value. There is a value to principle."

"I understand the words, but their meaning confuses me."

Connor smiled.

"There is meaning to everything. Everything has a meaning. There is a reason for everything that happens the way it does."

"I understand that. But why do you say this?"

"My family was murdered. But there is a reason for that. I don't understand the reason for my family bein' murdered, but I know there is a reason. The same can be said for the murder of your family."

"Yes. I have thought about that over many years. Sometimes I think I understand the reason. But then it turns to smoke and disappears. And with the smoke goes the good reason."

"I have to go find those five men. I have a reason for findin' 'em. Maybe it is just to find out what their reason was for murderin' my family. Maybe it is just to look in their eyes and have them understand my own reason for killin' 'em. I don't know any more why I'm doin' any of this. I wonder, am I that lost in the darkness that I can't find the path that leads me back to the light? Or is it my fate to wander forever without light to show me the way? Can you tell which it is?"

"If I could tell you, then perhaps I could find my own path," replied Geronimo. "But I am as lost as you. Don't tell my people that I am lost, because a leader cannot be lost. A leader must always know which path to follow."

"Yeah."

"Maybe I am no longer a leader. Maybe I should go with you and kill these bad men. Maybe then Usen will show me *my* path."

"I don't think it works that way."

"Maybe not. It was only a thought."

"I don't know how it actually works myself," said Connor.

"I have learned that there is nothing I can ever do in this life that will bring my family back to me. But I have also learned that if I do not turn away from those thoughts of revenge, I will surely lose myself in the darkness."

"For one who has lost everything, maybe darkness is all that's left."

"It is your sacred path, Connor Beckett. You must make the choices you need to make. When one rises up to see the light, I think it is foolish to duck back down into the darkness. But that is my belief — my philosophy. Yours maybe is different."

"Perhaps so. Perhaps not. But my answer, my path, lies somewhere out there, in the desert. I will not discover my path here. Tomorrow morning I will leave to discover that path — my answers."

Geronimo nodded somberly.

The morning sun was still an hour from raising its shining face over the horizon as Connor was cinching down Tilly's saddle.

The night before, there was a great discussion about allowing him to leave the camp with the knowledge of where it was located.

Geronimo spoke on Connor's behalf, but there were many voices raised against his leaving, for fear that he would tell the army where to find them.

The argument lasted until late into the night.

Finally, Geronimo came to Connor, smiled, and told him that he was free to leave without harm — that he had earned the trust of his people.

Connor stood alone in the middle of the camp. Good-byes had been said the night before.

He mounted Tilly and looked over the camp one last time, wondering if he would ever see these gentle people again, or if they, like him, would disappear into the desert sands and be lost to all forever.

On the outskirts of the camp was Stands Too Tall, already mounted on his pony, wearing a large pouch across his back. His rifle was in his right hand, the butt end resting on his thigh.

Connor halted Tilly in front of the brave.

"We did not say our good-byes last night."

"No need talk. I go with you."

"Why? This isn't your fight."

"Is for me to know why I go."

Connor nodded.

"Okay. Well, Stands Too Tall is welcome to travel with me for his own reason."

Stands Too Tall nodded. "We go now."

Connor looked behind him one last time and saw Geronimo standing in front of his lodge.

Their eyes locked on one another.

Connor raised his hand. Geronimo raised his. Connor and Stands Too Tall then turned their horses and rode off together, leaving the camp behind.

It took two full days for the duo to reach Buenavista from the Sonoran mountains, but time was no longer a consideration for Connor Beckett.

To prevent any accidents of misunderstanding, Stands Too Tall stayed hidden in the surrounding hills while Connor went into the small settlement to scout out what he could about the Brown Gang.

Thirty minutes later, a man on a galloping horse raced out of town toward the hills where Stands Too Tall was in hiding.

Connor's horse was in hot pursuit. And it was a well-aimed shot from Connor's rifle that felled the man from his saddle.

As Connor approached the man writhing in pain on the ground, holding onto his shoulder, he cocked his rifle and aimed it at him. Then he slid off his saddle and came to stand over him.

The last words spoken by Geronimo as they'd said their good-byes that last night rang in his ears: "Follow the light, not the darkness, Connor Beckett, and what you seek will be revealed."

Those words echoed loudly now in his brain. At the time he did not consider them important within the context of his immediate life, but now he heard them clearly. He understood every word, but he did not have the will to follow them. For now, he had men to track down and kill.

"Mister Heneford. I bet you thought you'd seen the last of me. You got any more of that kerosene?"

"I'm shot! You *shot* me!"

Connor bent over and moved the man's hand from the bullet wound. It was only a grazing wound.

"You're only nicked."

"Why did you shoot me?"

"Why did you run?"

"I wasn't gonna burn ya," replied Barlow Heneford, grimacing. "But that Cutter is one crazy son of a bitch. I woulda stopped him from doin' that, though. I wasn't gonna be party to no man burnin'. Ya gotta believe me."

"Yeah, I believe you, Barlow. Where are my horses?"

"They's all sold to others. Cutter unloaded them all soon as he arrived. Sorry."

"Where's Cutter now?"

"Oh, sorry, mister. I don't know. He cut out of here right after them Injuns attacked. He's long gone by now."

"That's too bad, Heneford. I was gonna let you live if you knew where he went. Now I guess there's no point in it."

Stands Too Tall rode up and slipped to the ground next to them.

"Oh, God! He with you?"

"He is. Stands Too Tall, this man don't know where Cutter is. I guess you can have him now. You gonna scalp him before you kill 'im? Or after?"

Stands Too Tall pulled his large steel knife from its sheath and grinned at Heneford.

"Wait!" said the terrified man. "Wait! I might know where he's headed. Yeah. I know where Cutter is headed."

"You do? You just said you didn't."

"It just come to me. It just come to me. He's headed down to Cananea."

"Where's Cananea?"

"Across the border. Two-days' ride."

"He went to Mexico?"

"Well, yes, sir. That's where Cananea is."

"I don't know if I trust what you're sayin' to be true. Stands Too Tall, do you know where Cananea is?"

"Is not far. Two-day ride, like he say."

Stands Too Tall then smiled.

"Why do you smile?" asked Connor.

"Cananea. Apache word for horsemeat. I am hungry now."

Connor smiled.

"Horsemeat? Ain't that somethin'. I guess I'm getting hungry myself now."

Connor turned his eyes back to Heneford.

"I think you might just be sayin' that to save yer skin, Barlow. I gotta remember not to tell people they're gonna live if they talk, 'cause then they go to tellin' me anything just to stay alive."

"No, sir. He's going down to Cananea. In fact, he's already there. He got himself a little señorita down in them parts. Goes by the name of Maria. Maria Eugenia Sanchez. He's got her set up in a little casa on the north end of the village. It's got a big yellow terra-cotta sun on the outside wall."

"Ain't you just a sudden wealth of knowledge. Terra-cotta sun, huh?"

"You can't miss it. That's where he is right now. I swear it."

Connor looked at Stands Too Tall.

"You believe his words?"

The Indian shook his head.

"He does not speak truth."

"Yes! Yes, I do. I'm tellin' ya, Cutter is there. Cutter is there. He's holed up in Cananea. I swear it on my life."

"Stands Too Tall, should we take the chance and let him go?"

"What if Cutter not there?"

"Then I guess we come back here and kill 'im."

The Indian nodded his agreement.

"No need you comin' back, mister. Cutter is there. He's there."

"Okay, Barlow. I believe you. Now there seems to be a matter of a missin' compatriot of yours. You know anything about 'im?"

"A missin' what?"

"The Apaches tell me there were eleven men at my cabin. I killed five of ya. The Apaches killed one. I believe that one was called Owen, if memory serves. That leaves five. Clay, Cutter, Earle, Flynn, that's four. That means there's one man missin'. Who's missin', Barlow?"

"I believe you're talkin' about Lloyd Baumgartner."

"Lloyd…?"

"Baumgartner. Lloyd Baumgartner."

"Okay. Where's Lloyd, Heneford?"

"He's dead."

"Dead? How'd he get himself dead?"

"Cutter shot 'im."

"Why did Cutter shoot Lloyd, Barlow?"

"Said he was cheatin' at cards. Cutter lost a real chunk one night here in Buenavista. Called Lloyd a cheat. Lloyd went for his gun, but Cutter was faster. It all happened the night before you came into the canyon."

"Well, Heneford, you might be tellin' me the truth, or you might be lyin' to me."

"I ain't lyin'. He's dead."

"I guess I'll have to take my chances with that. But don't worry, I won't be comin' back for ya."

"That's a relief."

Connor then shot Heneford in the forehead.

"We go Cananea?" asked Stands Too Tall.

"We go to Horsemeat."

CHAPTER 22

On the ride south to Cananea, Connor could not get Geronimo's many words of wisdom out of his head. *How could such a man be so misunderstood by so many?* The time spent with him, although short, had left an indelible impression on Connor. He understood Geronimo's purpose, he thought. The man was only trying to protect his people and preserve his way of life. What man wouldn't be willing to fight for that — be willing to kill for that — even be willing to die for that?

Stands Too Tall saw no need to disturb Connor's thoughts, for he was immersed in his own. Instead, they rode silently next to each other, each man knowing exactly where they were going, physically and metaphorically, and why. And they were headed straight for their own answers.

As the night settled in upon them, having no more need to conceal their presence, Connor and his trail mate sat close to the fire. Its warmth felt good. Its light made it easy for Connor to sit, think, and whittle on a small branch. Across from him sat Stands Too Tall, staring into the fire, lost within his own thoughts.

After some time, Connor stopped his whittling and looked up at the Indian.

"Goyahkla told me that your family was murdered same as mine."

Stands Too Tall nodded solemnly.

"I didn't want to ask you before because he said it is not polite to talk of the dead."

"Dead are dead, Connor Beckett. They in next world. They not care who speaks of them."

I didn't expect to hear that come from you. I thought all Apaches were of the same mind when it comes to the dead."

"All Apaches equal. But we not think same."

"The chief is not higher than a brave?"

"All have equal voice. Goyahkla is strong leader. Many think he right. Some think he wrong. But we all want live free. So we follow him to be free."

"So, on common ground you stand together."

"Freedom good."

"May I ask who killed your family?"

"Five White-Eyes."

"And you do not feel hate for all White-Eyes?"

"Some Apache bad. Some White-Eye bad. Five White-Eye kill family. They bad."

"When we are finished here, Stands Too Tall, I will help you find those who killed your family."

"They all dead."

"You kilt 'em?"

"No. Big snow kill them. I find them frozen in mountains."

"Froze to death? That's a tough way to go. Guess they deserved it, though. Do you still struggle with the hate?"

"I miss family. I miss smile on squaw's face when I return to her. I miss holding children in arms. But I not feel hate in my heart. I feel what Goyahkla feel in his heart now. I feel fear for losing freedom and way of life. It not our way to live only in one place, to hunt only in one place, to pray in place not sacred."

"Believe me, I understand. I didn't understand before. I thought it would be best for your kind to gather together, but I see now that the thinkin' is wrong on that issue. You should be free to do what you want to do. After all, that's why this country came into bein'. The first white folks didn't like bein' told what they could do either. It seems we ain't givin' your people the same freedom that the first white folks fought for."

"We cannot fight army. They too many. Too many rifles. We run now if we can, but I have fear we not run fast enough and far enough to escape what is to come for us."

"I'm afraid it's all gone too far for it to change now. The best your people can do, it seems, is simply survive the changes and adapt."

"I don't want to hear your words, Connor Beckett, but my heart hears your words. Your words are right, I think."

"If it means anything to you, after this affair is done and I find another place to call home, you and your people are welcome to share my land. I'd be proud to call you neighbors."

"This is why I ride with you. I see your skin is white, but you have heart and spirit of the People."

"Maybe you're right about that, 'cause right now I ain't feelin' too partial to the white ways myself. There's still four bad men out there somewhere, white as me, but I'm gonna kill 'em dead as can be despite the color of their skin."

"Hate still strong in you? I wish it not so."

"Yes, my friend. Goyahkla said the same. But I'm afraid it is. I can't seem to shake it none either." Connor pulled the small doll blanket from his shirt and stared at it. "My little girl didn't deserve what happened to her. None of my family deserved it. They never troubled no one. I think this is where most of the hatred hails from. I intend to let it all fly straight at those men when we find 'em. I intend for them to experience all the hate I can muster against 'em. Cutter has the doll my daughter was never without. He hangs onto it to keep the killin' alive in his heart. I intend to rip his heart out."

Connor picked up a small rock lying next to him and tossed it.

"We should catch up to the rest of 'em by tomorrow night, I reckon. Sooner, if we press a bit harder."

"Tomorrow hotter than today. We cannot go faster. Horses have no food."

"They were just fed in Buenavista."

"But sun strong. They already weak. We go to grass in hills."

"I suppose you're right. And if Heneford was right, Cutter is holed up in Cananea and thinks he's safe. I guess we ain't in no particular rush."

"They think you dead, Connor Beckett. They not in hurry. We find them soon. But if they together, they will have more guns."

"Yeah, but we have the advantage of surprise."

"Surprise or no surprise, if they see us first, they kill us."

"Look, my friend, I know you have your own reason for being here. But this really ain't your fight. I wouldn't hold it against you if you wanted to leave me here to fight this out myself."

"I will stay and reason still mine."

About an hour from sunrise, they were already under way. They headed for what Geronimo had called *las montañas bajas*, the lower hills, and fresh grazing land.

An hour after sunrise, the two sat on the ground as the horses ate their fill of fresh and wild blue grama grass. A small fire kept the morning chill from their bones, but in a couple of hours the fire would be too much for them.

"How far you reckon is Cananea?" asked Connor.

"Not far."

"Can we make there before dark?"

"After dark."

"Good. We'll give Cutter a wake-up call early in the mornin'. And then he'll die."

―――――⚬―――――

Connor tried to nap in the shade of a large rock outcrop next to a small spring of fresh water, but the afternoon heat made that impossible. Along with the unbearable heat, the visions of his dead family haunted him to fits of restlessness. He shuddered himself awake several times and finally surrendered to the visions and stood up. He stared out over the horses still grazing on the highly nutritious blue grama grass. They seemed contented.

He noted another shaded rock overlooking the valley below, and walked over to it. Sitting on the rock, he let his thoughts drift and soon found himself tracking the men in his mind. How he was going to get the drop on each of them. How he would put them to death. He even imagined the first shots of the gunfight. Of course, it might all go very differently: desperate men have been known to do unpredictably wild things after the sound of the first shot rings out.

He then realized that he also was one of the desperate men out here in the desert. His desperation might have been different, but it was leading him down a similar path. He wondered if his need for vengeance was a correct one. If his need was for justice, he might think differently. Revenge, he reasoned, was the heartless side of justice — akin to justice, but not justice. More like compensation.

Some might call it murder. They hung murderers in these parts. In any parts, actually. But then, murder was a legal term. So was justice.

Justice, it seemed, was for those who still consciously held a regard for the law. He was once one of those who held such a regard. Now, however, justice was too high a goal for his changed heart — too noble a thing for the blackness that was his hateful soul.

"*To the last, I grapple with thee; From Hell's heart, I stab at thee. For hate's sake, I spit my last breath at thee*," said Captain Ahab in one of Connor's favorite books, *Moby Dick*. If it was good enough for the good captain to shout so at a mere whale, then it was reason enough for him to shout it out at the despicable outlaw Cutter Brown. The law be damned. Justice be damned. Revenge be damned. He wanted Cutter Brown dead.

At that moment, he saw the whole affair become personal, and that changed everything. For he saw it just as Stands Too Tall had said earlier. The dead are dead. They have no concerns for the affairs of the living.

Stands Too Tall stirred. He rose to his feet and stretched and yawned. He twisted around until he saw Connor sitting on the rock.

He walked toward Connor as if deeply disturbed about something.

Connor turned his head and looked into the Indian's eyes.

"The problem with a good sleep," he said, "is that it ends too soon, and the beautiful visions from your best dreams become the horrific sights too terrible to be real to your awakened eyes. But then such is the deception of fantasy."

Stands Too Tall shook his head. "I not understand all your words, but pictures with eyes closed better than with eyes open, I think."

"I couldn't have said it better myself."

"We go. I think it good night to ride."

"I've never ridden in the dark. Always been afraid my horse would break a leg in a varmint hole."

"Horses know how to walk in dark. We sit and think other thoughts."

"Okay. If you say so. Besides, if the ride gets me closer to the man who needs killin', it *will* be a good night."

"Horses strong again. We push them. We see man you seek after sun gone."

"Sounds like a worthy ride to me."

"Hate still strong in your heart?"

"It is."

"I wish it not so, Connor Beckett."

"I know, I know. But wishing, it seems these days, don't make things so." Connor slid down off the rock. "Let's make ready. We got a long ride ahead of us."

CHAPTER 23

With the sweltering heat of the day having given over to the brisk chill of the following night, the two men rode on. A blanket around Stands Too Tall and a coat worn by Connor were all that kept the chill from their bones, but the cool air allowed the horses to lope easily. They were traveling quickly.

The ride during the previous night had also allowed them to move very quickly. Though they'd had to slow their pace to get through the day, that day was now behind them.

Connor guessed it to be near nine or ten o'clock when Stands Too Tall reined his horse to a stop and slipped off the horse and onto the ground in one smooth move.

"What is it? Why we stopping?" asked Connor, halting his horse next to the Apache.

The Indian pressed an index finger to his lips.

"You hear?" he whispered.

Connor strained his ears to hear. "I don't hear nothin'."

"You not have ears of Apache. Stay here." Stands Too Tall handed his reins to Connor. "I will return."

Connor glanced around him, but the black night still presented only the empty vision of darkness. Even the bright starlight seemed too dark on this night. Stands Too Tall slipped away into that darkness, leaving Connor to hold the horses and stare dumbly out into the night.

***

About fifteen minutes later, Stands Too Tall returned.

"What took you so long?" whispered Connor. "What is it? What did you see?"

"Two men by fire outside adobe casa. I see yellow sun on side. They awake and have rifles."

"How can you see anything out here?"

"You not have eyes of Apache. But in light of fire it not hard to see two men, Connor Beckett."

"Okay, okay. It seems I don't have the humor of the Apaches either.

Stands Too Tall smiled.

"Two men, huh?" asked Connor. "Must be sentries for Cutter."

"Yes. I look horses' marks in dirt. I know marks of horses same. Horses from your ranch. Both men sick. One empties belly into sand. Empty bottle at feet."

"Drunk sick, I reckon. I wouldn't worry myself about them, then. They ain't gonna live long enough to get sober."

"We kill them?"

"We do. I'll take the first shot."

"No. Rifle too loud. One inside casa run away." Stands Too Tall pulled his knife from its leather sheath. "I kill them and come back."

"No!" said Connor. "It was *my* family. I claim the right to kill them."

The Indian nodded and replaced his knife in its sheath.

Connor pulled his own knife out and held it up in front of his face. He could see the reflection of the stars overhead on the shiny blade.

"You think I can get close enough to 'em to use this?"

Stands Too Tall nodded. "If you quiet like Apache. Fire high. Your white eyes see them. They much sick from bottle. Will be easy to kill."

"Then that's what I'm gonna do — kill 'em."

Connor skulked away.

Connor crept closer to the casa. All he could see from his position behind a large boulder were two silhouettes on the ground on opposite sides of a campfire. Both men were teetering back and forth and slurring words in the midst of some half-baked conversation that he couldn't quite make out.

In his mind flashed a vision of his family's surprised faces as these men forced their way into their home. He saw his wife immediately reach for her children to try and protect them by shielding them with her body.

That was the spark he needed to re-ignite the searing blaze of rage. He then invented a vision of how one of these men, whose face was hidden by the brim of his hat, might have approached his stricken family and punched his wife in the jaw so hard that it sent her sprawling to the floor unconscious and unable to defend her children.

From the welts and bruises on her face the day he found her, he could tell that she had suffered repeated blows from hardened fists. From there, it was a simple thing for him to infer the deed of the clouting to either one of these men, or to both. But it didn't matter to him if neither of these men had struck his wife; they were guilty by association. That was good enough for him.

It was now easy for him to hate them equally — with a hate so fully reborn of fury and spite as to justify anything he might do to them. But he feared that there would be no time to delve into his torturous fantasies. Cutter was inside and Connor could not risk his escape while he, Connor, dabbled about indulging his torturous desires, especially knowing that his daughter's little doll was being kept as a sick memento by a perverted beast. He wished he would have the time to make their last hours as torturous as possible, but he accepted that a quick kill might be all he could achieve.

Geronimo's face flashed before his mind's eye and then his rich voice followed.

"Your eyes are crazy with the great hate. Therefore, I shall call you Crazy-Eyes until your heart changes and the crazy is gone, and I can call you by a

better name. My hope is to change your name before it is too late."

Wise Geronimo was right. The crazy had rekindled and it burned hot — white hot. And his eyes were blinded by its brightness.

"I'm not ready to forgive or forget," whispered Connor in his imagined response to Geronimo. "I need to keep hold of the fury a while longer. I need it. I NEED it!"

And then, as if to confirm his belief, he pushed the image of his tortured and abused family to the front of his brain. That was what he needed to get him fully motivated. His mind revisited the thoughts of torturing the two drunken beasts.

Geronimo's other words then flashed through him, *"A lover may depart, but love remains. I think it would be better for you to look for the love that remains and not the hate."* Such words, spoken by a man who understood the nature of hate so well gave him a second's pause to wonder if he was on the correct path — this destructive path.

But before such an internal conflict could alter his purpose, he pushed everything that was not hate, not anger, not rage, to the back of his mind. He would not, he *could* not be persuaded from his bloody task.

Perhaps, in the end, love would prove stronger than hate, but not today — not today!

For the demon he had become, love was impossible. He returned his thoughts to carving up the two men.

He stared at his knife and shook his head. A quick death from the stab of his blade was too kind, he argued to himself. In fact, he regretted killing that first outlaw with a bullet from his rifle. He'd gotten off much too easy.

The conflict continued within his brain until he reasoned it out that he had to force himself to disband from the idea of torture and concentrate on capturing Cutter. Thus, regarding those two drunken animals, whatever he wanted to do to them had to be resolved with a quick and sure thrust of his knife.

He considered then, to his chagrin, that despite all his hopes and wishes, he possessed no more torturous tools than a heavy chunk of stone, which ultimately would prove to be no different from a knife thrust or a bullet.

Then a sounder thought rushed in. These drunk men were not his goal. Anything he might conjure up against them would only be a pretense to his ultimate goal of capturing and brutalizing Cutter Brown. After all, it was Cutter Brown who prompted him to be here.

He readied himself. He knew what he was going to do. He shifted the knife back to his right hand and moved toward the weaving men, keeping as quiet as a mouse.

The dancing firelight against the casa gave an eerie feel to his approach as each carefully placed step of his boot brought him closer to the men. Stands Too Tall was right; if he could remain silent on his approach, the men wouldn't know what hit them as he plunged his knife into the backs of their heads, creating instant rag dolls.

By the time Connor had gotten into position, the two men had fallen asleep sitting up. He realized his initial task had been made much easier. But then a light sparked into being inside the cabin.

With the nearest man now only about five feet ahead of him, he reached out his left hand, readying it to slap it over the man's mouth to prevent him from crying out and alerting Cutter Brown.

He crept closer and closer until the sleeping man's head was only a foot away. He began trembling. The trembling grew into a paralyzing panic, but he fought through it. He was only inches away from clasping his hand over the man's mouth when the image of his young daughter filled his mind. She was reeling in horror and shaking her head. He could almost hear the words she mouthed in silence. "No, Papa! No!"

He was unable to discern her meaning. Was she reacting to the threat of the outlaws, calling out for her papa to save her? Or was she hoping to stop Connor from advancing his agenda against the sleeping men?

He blinked and the vision disappeared. Despite the confusion created by the vision, he was suddenly re-filled with an unbounded rage and loathing.

His left hand shot forward and he clasped it over the mouth of the man. At the same time, he jammed the point of his knife into the man's neck at the base of his skull.

The man's body went limp. He withdrew the knife and gently laid the man's head back against the rock he had been sitting up against.

The second man remained asleep and so he moved his foot in that man's direction.

The snap of the twig under his foot was loud enough to rouse the sleeping man. His head cocked up. Their eyes met. The man's eyes widened in both recognition and alarm.

"He's here!" he shouted just before Connor could close the gap between them and stab his knife into the man's throat, silencing him.

It was too late, however. Connor instantly heard a commotion from inside the casa. Someone was thrashing about wildly.

He stepped up to the door and pulled his revolver as shots were fired from inside the house. A bullet ripped through the wood and then through Connor's left shoulder, knocking him to the ground.

Wounded and woozy, he heard glass breaking at the side of the house. His head fell heavily forward and then he slipped into a dark silence.

Connor's eyes opened, but they wandered about in his head as if they had no point upon which to focus.

A hand reached down and lightly smacked his face. His eyes began to focus.

"What happened?" he asked.

A familiar face appeared. It was Stands Too Tall.

"You try go next world."

"I tried what?"

"For ten suns you try cross over, but you no go. You stay this world."

"Ten… You're sayin' I've been out for ten *days*? I must have been battling an infection."

Connor tried to sit up, but the excruciating pain in his left shoulder knocked him onto his back. He reached for his shoulder and made painful contact with it.

"Have I been shot?"

Stands Too Tall nodded.

"You horse travel well with you over saddle."

"Where am I?"

Another familiar face appeared. It was Geronimo's.

"Am I back at camp?"

"We are at a different camp. But you are back with us."

"I don't remember gettin' shot."

"It is good you do not remember. You howled like Coyote for days."

Then flashes of memory returned.

"A gunfight. I was in some kinda gunfight."

"Yes. In Cananea."

It all came back to him in a rush.

"Cutter! I was at the door. Did he shoot me?"

"Yes. He shot through the door."

"Damn! That was stupid of me to stand in front of the door."

Geronimo nodded.

"Usen does not have need of you right now. That is why you are still here, I think."

"What of Cutter?"

"You need to think about healing first," said Geronimo. "There will be time later to think about him."

"I had him and I let him get away. How stupid of me!"

"You have almost given your all to this task," said Geronimo. "I can see this."

"I'm not done yet. I'm committed to my task, mind and body, heart and soul."

"When this is over, Connor Beckett, what will be left of your mind and body, your heart and your soul?"

"I ain't thought that far ahead."

"You should think about it now, before you become lost in the darkness of your hate."

"My philosophy of hate?"

"What of philosophy? It seems to me that philosophy is just silly words spoken by silly people for silly reasons that have nothing to do with real life."

"Maybe so, Goyahkla."

"Tell me, Connor Beckett. You have killed more men now. Is your family back with you?"

"No, they ain't. But…"

"Is your heart lighter?"

"No. Not really."

"Has a song returned to your voice?"

"No."

"Has your life gotten any better for you?"

"I know what you're sayin', but…"

"Have you found your freedom?"

"I'll never find…"

"Have you created good artwork for your life?"

"No. I don't see no kinda art at all."

"It was white men that killed your family. Do you now hold hate for all white men?"

"No. Men are both good and bad. The color of their skin does not determine this. What lies in the head, the heart, and the spirit make a man what he is."

"Who are you, Connor Beckett?"

"I…"

"Do not answer yet. Sleep. Rest. Restore your health. We will speak on all of this another time."

CHAPTER 24

Connor had been left alone with his thoughts for several hours when Geronimo walked up to him. He pulled his hand from behind his back. In it was the cloth doll of Connor's daughter.

"Rebecca!" said Connor.

Geronimo handed the doll over.

"Does this heal your heart, Connor Beckett? Does this quiet the rage?"

Connor clutched the doll to his chest and closed his eyes.

"Where did you get this?"

"Stands Too Tall picked it up at the casa in Cananea on the night you were shot."

"Why didn't he tell me he had it?"

"I told him not to tell you. You were not ready to see it. Maybe you are ready now. Are you? Are you ready now?"

"I don't know. I like to think so."

"Then I ask you again. Does this heal your heart? Does this quiet the rage?

"Some, I guess."

"Some? Not all?"

"Some. Yes. Thank you, Goyahkla. Thank you."

"But are you ready?"

"Ready for what?"

"Ready to walk away from your hate."

"I don't know."

"When you know, tell me."

Geronimo turned to walk away.

"Wait!"

Geronimo turned back to Connor.

"The doll means much to me and I'm very grateful for it. But how do I walk away from the hate, like you have?"

"One step at a time, Connor Beckett. You already know this."

"Yes. But how did *you* do it?"

"I could not find all the Mexicans that killed my family. I searched for many years, but they had disappeared into history. I could not follow them to that place. It is too far for me in this life. I had to let them go so I could live."

"But if you could find them now, what would you do?"

"Now, Connor Beckett, I would touch them on the head. I would count my coup. And I would walk away from them. I would live my life."

"You wouldn't kill them?"

"I have said this many times already and still you do not hear me. When your ears are open, I will tell you one more time."

"They're open. I can hear."

"Can you truly hear me? Can you hear the truth?"

"I can."

"Then I will tell you one last time. I shall not say this ever again."

"Okay. I'm listening."

"Will killing them bring my family back to me?"

"No. I reckon not. But why would you let them live? Why wouldn't you kill them if you could?"

"My soul is already black enough from all the killing I did. I do not wish to darken it more. More darkness means more weight to carry. I'm old. I do not wish to carry the weight any longer."

"But then they got away with murder."

"But I did not change."

"What does that mean?"

"I have given up the need to kill them so I could remain myself. I could search for them. And maybe I would find them all, if they are not already dead. And maybe I could kill them all. I still would not have my family back, but I would now be *them*. I would become their hate. I would not be myself. I would have lost the battle with the evil ones to keep who I am. And who I am is the one who cares for my people. Who tries to keep my people free and safe. Would I do that if I changed and became only the hate of them who murdered my family?"

"I see that now!"

"Then do you now hear the truth of my words?"

"Yes. I hear you."

"Then I ask again. Is the doll enough for you? Does it quiet the rage? Does it bring light to your spirit?"

"It helps, yes."

"Can you walk away from all the killing? Can you leave the weight of death behind?"

"I don't honestly know, Goyahkla. Cutter is out there somewhere. At peace and not caring about what he has done."

"He does not live in peace. He does not sleep in peace. He will always look behind him."

"I suppose so."

"He will have to live with what he has done. He will have to carry the weight of his evil."

"Yeah. I see that."

"Tell me, Connor Beckett. Can you live with what you have done? Can you carry the weight of your evil?"

"Not for long, I guess. I will have to lose the weight to live. I see that now."

"Can you live with that?"

"I can live with that. I suppose he'll face his own justice sooner or later."

"Those are good words. I like those words. But do they come from the heart, or are they words you think I would like to hear?"

"Those are words from my heart, Goyahkla."

"If you should ever find him, what will you do?"

"I would touch his head and count coup. I would walk away from the weight of his blackness. I would lighten my heart for my walk along my own sacred path."

"I wish I could believe your words. I like those words. They are strong words. They have great meaning for you."

"I speak my truth. I do not lie."

Geronimo turned and waved to some braves standing a good distance away.

Within minutes two braves dragged a third man toward Connor.

Instantly, he recognized the man as Cutter Brown.

His face flushed with blood. His mind seized up. He couldn't think. His fingers clenched into hard fists. He looked skyward and screamed loudly. He dropped the doll to the sand.

Cutter Brown was brought before Connor and dropped to the ground in front of him.

Connor was handed a large steel knife. He grasped the handle and stared down at Cutter Brown grinning up at him from the ground.

"Go on and do it, Beckett. Go ahead. You earned it. You win. But I ain't gonna say I'm sorry. You ain't gonna hear me beg for my life neither. I'd do it again, if I could. I enjoyed your girls. I really did. I had me a good time with 'em. Is that what you want to hear? No?"

Cutter laughed.

Rage surged through Connor's body, but he held his ground. He did not surrender to every intense instinct that told him to plunge the knife into Cutter Brown's throat to silence his taunting.

"Do you hear me, Beckett? I'd do it again and again and again, if I could. I enjoyed it. I revel in the memory of my deed. I ain't never gonna apologize for what I did. I just want to keep the memory of it fresh in my head. Now kill me, you coward. Go back to Tombstone and read your newsprint. Go have a nice relaxin' drink. Don't take no thought of leavin' yer next family alone on yer ranch. Go relax. Go have yerself a good time. Your little wife told me all about yer day of rest and how you liked to leave 'em and go have yer fancy. You ain't no kinda husband. You ain't no kinda father. You're just a selfish bastard and that's why yer family was left to my doin's. You deserved it, Beckett. Now kill me, you coward, you selfish bastard."

Connor could take no more and screamed at Cutter.

SHUT UP! SHUT UP! YOU SHUT YOUR DAMN DIRTY MOUTH, YOU SON OF A BITCH!"

Connor leapt at him and got behind the outlaw. He grabbed his hair and jerked his head backward, exposing the killer's throat.

"Do it, Beckett. I ain't never gonna say I'm sorry. Never!"

Connor shook from the fury within him. He stared down into the dead eyes of the outlaw. But he withheld his blade from the killer's throat.

Cutter saw the hesitation in his eyes.

"Give me mercy, then. Kill me. Don't leave me with these redskins. Kill me! Kill me!"

"You kilt my whole family, you son of a bitch. Don't go askin' mercy from me. You ain't got no right to mercy."

"Kill me! Kill me, you gutless coward. You weren't no father to them kids. You weren't no husband to that fine sweet woman. You let them die so's you could enjoy yourself in town."

Connor looked skyward and screamed until his face was red as blood.

"Kill me!" screamed Cutter.

But Connor was frozen.

"Your wife, I think she liked what I did to her. I think she was enjoyin' it a lot. She pushed back against me."

"SHUT UP!"

Cutter Brown had run out of taunting words. He just closed his eyes tight.

"Kill me, Beckett," he whispered.

Connor brought the knife closer to the rapist's throat and then looked up at Geronimo. The old chief sat motionless, expressionless, with unblinking eyes.

Connor looked deep into the face so like his own. Then he smacked the flat side of the blade against the crown of Cutter Brown's head.

"No. I will not surrender to you. I will not become you. I count coup upon you, Cutter Brown. Go find the peace of your death somewhere else. You'll not get me to carry the weight of your blackness."

Connor released the outlaw's hair and stepped away from him. He turned the knife around and laid its handle into Stands Too Tall's hand.

"Nothing I do will bring my family back to me. I choose to walk my path lighter. I choose to be me."

Stands Too Tall smiled and nodded.

"It be good walk, I think."

"Only time will tell, my friend."

Connor walked over and stood in front of Geronimo.

"I claim victory. I choose to live, and be me, and tell my story."

Geronimo smiled.

"I think it will be a good story. And I see a great artist who has created the good artwork of living."

"I won my life back," said Connor.

"You've won nothing," said Cutter Brown.

"Perhaps," replied Connor. "But *you've* lost everything."

Geronimo made a hand gesture to Stands Too Tall. The Apache warrior immediately walked to Brown and severed his bindings.

The outlaw stood up, rubbing his wrists.

"What's this?"

"You should run now, evil one," said Geronimo. "Run with the life that Connor Beckett has given back to you."

"Run? Hell, yeah, I'll run. But you ain't seen the last of me, Beckett. You'll see me again and again. If not in the flesh, then in your dreams. Sleep good, Beckett. You'll need it."

And Brown ran away down the slope of the mountainside as fast as he could.

Connor picked up the doll, dusted it off, and pressed it against his chest. He stared at the receding figure of the outlaw, his face empty of all emotion.

"You're the one who's gonna have to find some way to sleep," he said in a hushed voice.

Geronimo gestured again.

Stands Too Tall pulled an arrow from his quiver, nocked the arrow to the string of his bow, aimed it, steadied his arm, and let the arrow go.

Seconds later, the arrow struck the outlaw in the back. He fell instantly to the sandy ground, sliding face first to a halt next to a large boulder. He did not move. He was dead.

Geronimo nodded.

"Why?" asked Connor. "I spared his life. I did not want his death to blacken my spirit."

"His death is not your burden," said Geronimo.

"But…"

"I claim his death."

"Why?"

"He knew this location. He might tell the army where we are. I could not allow him to do that. You can walk lighter, Connor Beckett. His blackness will be mine to carry."

"How do I thank you, Goyahkla?"

"There is no need to thank me. I do what I must to protect my people."

CHAPTER 25

Connor tightened the cinch of Tilly's saddle as Geronimo walked up behind him.

"I asked you to choose for me," said Geronimo. "Life on the reservation or continue fighting. You told me to choose life so that I might tell my story. And now you have chosen the same for yourself."

"I suppose I have. But what are you gonna do about your feelings for the White-Eye? They will come to your land as blades of grass to the prairie."

"They can come. They are stronger than we are. I see now that the land no longer belongs to everyone. That some will claim pieces of it for themselves. Those who are stronger than those who are weaker. I think this will be the future. It is not a good thing, but it is what it will be."

"The hate in you is truly gone for the White-Eye?"

"It is not for the White-Eye that I feel hate. I have already told you this. My hate is for the philosophy of all men who wish to force their understanding of what is to be and what is not to be upon others who cannot stand and shout with a great loud voice their outrage for what is being done to them. I wanted to live free. But I run away and hide now. That is not freedom. I have wanted nothing more than to live the life I was meant to live — free to be who I was meant to be. That is gone now. I can only be who I am *allowed* to be. This angers me. But my anger is hollow. And I do not have the strength to resist much longer. My rage is old, too. It does not have the teeth it once had. This land will never be the same. I will never be the same. I did not want this change, but it is here now. It is what life has become."

"'*I am damned for wanting,*'" said Connor. "I heard a man say that once. '*For wanting to live in the purity of truth. For wanting to live in harmony with all things. For wanting to believe in a justice system that fails to live within the hearts of those who dispense it so callously and with so much certainty. For the wanting of all good things in this cruel world, I am forever damned.*'"

"Wanting should not be an evil thing," said Geronimo. "I think the world is very complicated, but as I have said already, I believe it is not necessary to complicate your life to accomplish your life."

"I like those words. To shed that which is not needed is a good way to live, I think."

Geronimo smiled and then continued.

"One day a man gathered together all his problems and wrapped them in a bundle. He walked to the river's edge. He tossed the bundle into the river and watched as it was swept away from him by the fast water.

"'I am done with all my problems,' he said. 'I have sent them all away. Now I am free of all problems.'

"Just then a bundle of belongings washed ashore next to him. He picked up the bundle and was pleased with what he saw. And he took the bundle home with him.

"Downstream, along the river's edge, a long way from where the man had stood, another man picked up a bundle of things that looked good to him. He took them home and was happy."

Connor waited for more, but Geronimo had finished his story.

"So...each man threw his problems into the river. But someone else saw his problems not as problems, but as something nice to have. Is that right?"

Geronimo looked at him and said nothing.

"Is that right?" asked Connor again.

"Is that what the story means to you?"

"I guess so."

"A man chooses to hear and see what he wants to hear and see. It is for him alone to judge a thing as good or bad. That is how one must look upon change. It might be good or it might be bad. It is for each one alone to decide."

"My heart remains wounded. I expect it will take time to heal completely, but I have stopped stabbing it. And so it should heal."

Geronimo smiled and nodded.

"Perhaps I will stop stabbing mine soon and allow it to heal also."

"Perhaps you will. When you are ready to accept the healing."

"Your words are from the mind of a holy man."

"I'm certainly not that. But I'm not what I was a short time ago either. I will miss you all very much."

Geronimo nodded.

Stands Too Tall then walked up to Connor.

"Stands Too Tall. I was going to find you," continued Connor, "I can never repay you for saving my life. All I can do for now is say thank you."

"That is enough," replied the Apache brave.

"Goyahkla. You saved my life and my spirit. The fire is gone. The heat of my hate has turned to only a warm breeze. In time I hope it will grow cold and my shouts of rage become a song. I will never forget 'The One Who Yawns,' for he helped me to quiet my terrors and to sleep calmly again. Thank you, my very good friend."

"I think I shall not see you again, and my heart is heavy with that thought," said Geronimo. "I have not the words to stop the tears that fall within my heart for you. In a very short time, we have traveled far, you and I, on the path we have chosen to walk together for a time. But that time, like a river, has moved on and I shall miss our talks. When the fire of my life is gone and Usen comes to lift me into forever, I shall speak kindly of you. I shall look in on you from time to time and see if your spirit has remained calm. I hope it will be so."

"I *will* see you again, Goyahkla. You can count on it. Someday, wherever you are, I will show up and we will speak again."

"I hope by then, Connor Beckett, I will have driven the army crazy and they will have stopped chasing me and let me live my life as I choose. But until then, I want to make them crazier."

Connor chuckled.

"And you're just the one to do it, too."

Connor mounted Tilly and shortened the reins.

"Where will you go?" asked Geronimo.

"First I will go to my ranch and bury this doll in my daughter's grave. Then I will go to my father's home. I need to speak with him and my brothers about many things."

"I shall ask Usen to protect you on your path."

"I'll take all the help I can get. And as a man named Byron once wrote, '*Fare thee well. And if forever, still forever, fare thee well.*'

And Connor Beckett, restored to whole form and forever grateful, reined Tilly away from the camp, wondering what would become of the great man he knew as friend, Goyahkla, master of his own philosophy.

EPILOGUE

After several more meetings wherein I came to know Geronimo much better, I met with him in a saloon just off the reservation in Lawton, Oklahoma, for the final time on the night of February 15, 1909.

The old chief greeted me warmly. We hugged as friends this time.

We sat and spoke of our time together during all my informal interviews. I thanked him again for allowing me to read the journal written by Connor Beckett, and for the kind and comforting words he spoke to me every time we parted company.

Geronimo was already well intoxicated by the time I arrived for our scheduled meeting, but we sat together and had a few more just for the sake of old times and familiar faces. And we conversed not as reporter and interviewee, but as friends.

"So tell me," I said, "why did you really give yourself to General Miles at Skeleton Canyon back in eighty-six?"

"I could run no more and I finally lost my fear," said Geronimo with a sad smile.

"The fear of not living free?"

"The fear that my people would never live free again."

"You're still not afraid of captivity, then?"

"My people live, Gerald Thompson. In captivity or free on the plains, in the mountains, or in the desert, it does not matter anymore. Those days have fallen into the dust of the old world. My people live. That is enough for me in this moment."

"What of Stands Too Tall, Goyahkla?"

"He died in Florida, at Fort Marion."

"I'm sorry to hear that."

"I am sorry for many things, Gerald Thompson."

"Regrets, Goyahkla. Do you have any regrets?"

"Every day that a man holds on to regrets, he misses the wonder of that day. He misses the hope of that day. Regrets, just like hate, anger, and rage, all of them carried in your heart, are too heavy for the walk on your sacred path. They should be dropped and left behind. Yes, it is better, I think, to walk your sacred path with a light heart."

"So you have no regrets at all?"

"I have only one, and it is of great weight."

"What is that, my friend?"

"I regret surrendering."

"You can admit that now?"

"It does not matter what I admit to anymore."

"But when we first met, you told me you didn't surrender. You told me you made a choice between fighting the army and wanting your people to live."

Geronimo smiled.

"I was younger then."

"It was only three months ago."

"I'm older now. I'm wiser. It was a surrender."

"And you do regret surrendering?"

"I do."

"Can you drop that regret and walk your path with a lighter heart?"

"For now, no, but I am trying to learn how I might do that."

"Somewhere between Hell and breakfast?"

Geronimo smiled again.

"Yes, somewhere in between."

Sometime later, Geronimo told me that he'd had enough to drink and was going to ride his horse a few miles back to his home.

"Can you find your way okay?" I asked.

Geronimo chuckled.

"The horse knows the way home."

I asked him if I should accompany him back to his house just to be safe, but the old man refused my offer.

"I have come this far in my life on my own. I think I can make it back to my house without any help."

"Don't fall off your horse, old man," I said teasingly.

Geronimo smirked again. "I am an Indian. Indians do not fall from their horses."

I chuckled.

"I'm going down to the Brazos, to meet with Connor Beckett. I'll stop back on my way up from Texas and visit you in a few weeks."

"Tell him that I still think of him and that I hope he found what he was looking for."

"I most certainly will. I'm looking for something new myself. I quit my newspaper job. I don't exactly know what I'm looking for at the moment, but I hope to find it soon."

"What you are looking for," said Geronimo, "is also looking for you. And one day it will find you. I hope what you are looking for is a good thing."

"I hope so, too, my friend. I hope so, too."

Geronimo nodded, turned, and walked away. He stopped. His sudden halt caught my attention. He turned to me. "If I *should* fall from my horse on this night, I think I shall fall completely through the earth and land in the next world."

I smiled.

Without another word or gesture, my good friend, Goyahkla, The One Who Yawns, turned and walked away. We never met again.

<hr/>

I did, however, meet with Connor Beckett and he gave me his permission to edit his story and recite it herein. And after reconciling with his father and brothers, he bought a ranch of his own — along the Brazos, living alone with his many memories, but without any regrets. Without any hate. Without any rage. With a heart finally healed and a song upon his lips.

After I returned from that meeting, I found what *I* had been looking for — what had been looking for me also. And I wrote this book.

As my aged native friend told me during our first meeting, *"there is an art to living. And we are the artists who create the artwork on the canvas that is our life."*

I like to think, during times of deeper reflection, that somewhere, somewhere between Hell and breakfast, I have become a good artist and that my canvas is agreeably represented. But I suppose that judgment must be left to those artists who might speak of me after I have ended my own sacred walk. My only hope is that they will be good words, spoken graciously on behalf of this humble artist.

The greatest artist I've ever known, Goyahkla, also known as Geronimo, rode off into history that evening of our last meeting and into the pages of legend. He *did* fall from his horse on that fateful ride home and lay on the road, in a puddle, all night long. As a result, he contracted pneumonia, to which he succumbed on February 17, 1909.

So in a way his fall did land him in the next world, as he had predicted. And I am told that the landing came about sometime after breakfast.

~ Gerald Curtis Thompson
1910

THE END

Wisdom of Goyahkla

Our past never leaves us. It remains with us always, as a part of us — a part of who we eventually become.

I have lost my freedom. But had I always remained free, I would not now appreciate the value of its loss.

Lost is something only to be found through misfortune.

Depending on why a battle is fought, it might be argued that there could be a more terrible loss to be found in victory and a greater gain found in defeat. But that argument belongs only to the victor.

ABOUT THE AUTHOR

Dillon Garrison (Val Edward Simone) was born in Seattle, Washington, and has been writing since 1980.

Val has published adult-themed action/adventure novels; historical fiction; western novels; short stories; a collection of thoughts, musings, and observations; a collection of children's short stories; and several children's picture books. He continues to work on many other novels, short stories and screenplays.

He is also a strong advocate of early childhood development through the arts, and continues to support all efforts toward helping children discover their own creativity through reading, writing, and drawing.

Val currently lives and writes in Arizona.

His websites:
Ekidsland Publishing
Morningside Publishing
Ekidsland (For kids only)

Connect with Val Online:
Twitter: @valsimone
Instagram: @valedwardsimone
Linkedin: Val Edward Simone

Other Books by Val Edward Simone
Novels/Novellas
Blood Trackers: One Crazy Love Story
Blood Trackers 2: Revenge of an Angel
About Things I Lost Long Ago…scribblings from a foolish heart
The Wondrous Life of a Long-Ago Man
Comes the Devil to Crooked Creek
Captain Delightable's Magical Tales of a Minchon Warrior
A Minute of Forever
Into the Light Boldly…an odyssey of self-discovery
The Firestone…Is Mankind Ready?
The Story
Adventures at Dead River

Short Stories
Manifest Destiny
The Secret Life of Goner Andling
Love Bytes
Dragons Within
The Problem with Dragons
The Unfortunate Dragon
The Fairy Collection
Through the Waterfall
Fairy Forgotten
Emily's Wish
Kaylee's Secret
The Wizard of Sebastianville

Children's Picture Books
Felix
The Gingerbread Pony
The Littlest Bell
Mean Muley McGrudge
Otto and Kevin
Proton Gator
Sammy Sparrow Spy

Children's Coloring Book
Proton Gator & Friends Coloring Book